DATE DUE

W9-AUG-752

Reconceptions in Christian Thinking

1817-1967

W. NORMAN PITTENGER

The Seabury Press • New York

Copyright © 1968 by The Seabury Press, Incorporated
Library of Congress Catalog Card Number: 68–11591
Design by Bennett Robinson Company
588-168-C-3
Printed in the United States of America

Preface

The chapters of this book were originally delivered as the Paddock Lectures at the General Theological Seminary, New York City, in November, 1967, and formed a part of the observance of the 150th anniversary of its founding.

When, several years ago, Lawrence Rose, who at that time was Dean of the Seminary, invited me to deliver the Paddock Lectures in 1967, he suggested that a suitable topic on such an occasion would be "what has happened theologically during the past hundred and fifty years." The suggestion seemed sound, and I began to think of ways in which the subject could be treated. At first, I thought of a quasi-historical study of the period, with special attention to Anglican divinity. But I rejected this idea at once, not only because I can make no claim to being a historian but also because there are already several excellent books which cover either all or the more significant parts of the period in question. Vernon F. Storr's *Development of English*

3

Religious Thought, 1800–1860, and its continuation in L. E. Elliott-Binns's *English Thought, 1860–1900,* at once come to mind; and for the period from 1900 to recent years, J. K. Mozley's *Some Tendencies in Recent British Theology* and A. M. Ramsey's *From Gore to Temple,* not to mention the admirable little work by A. R. Vidler, *Twentieth-Century Defenders of the Faith,* are readily available for students. Next, I considered the possibility of a study of the influential Anglican divines of the period 1817–1967. It might have been interesting to discuss Maurice, Church, Hort, Westcott, Gore, DuBose in the United States, William Temple, and A. E. Taylor, for example, in an attempt to evaluate their contributions to theology. But most of these men have already been the subject of books or significant essays; and in any event, this kind of biographical approach did not seem exactly my *métier.*

So, finally, I decided to devote the lectures to the consideration of what appear to me important *topics.* A discussion of topics is certainly *topical,* which would seem to be desirable in a series of relatively popular lectures. Furthermore, this sort of study is more to my own inclination, since my interest over many years has been in theology in its wider philosophical implications rather than in its historical (or biblical) background and development—although I hasten to add that I should be the last person to wish to discount these. Finally, the kind of treatment which this method demands makes possible, in each instance, a direct presentation of one possible interpretation of the issue; and perhaps that is not a useless enterprise. Whether I have chosen wisely is not for me to say, but I may express the hope that the lectures were to some degree informative and suggestive, and perhaps now and again provocative.

Preface

It remains for me to express once again my gratitude to the Very Reverend Lawrence Rose, former Dean of the General Seminary, and to the members of the Paddock Lectureship Committee for their invitation; and to thank the present Dean, the Very Reverend Samuel J. Wylie, his wife, the members of the faculty of the Seminary, and the students and guests who so kindly listened to the lectures, for all that they did to make my fortnight in Chelsea Square so pleasant and rewarding. The General Seminary has had a distinguished history; I am honored that I myself could have spent more than thirty years making some small contribution to its life, as instructor and then professor of apologetics there. I speak for thousands when I express the hope that its next 150 years will be as significant in the life of the Episcopal Church in the United States, in the Anglican Communion throughout the world, and in the whole ecumenical Church of Christ, as its first 150 years have been.

King's College,   *Norman Pittenger*
Cambridge, England

Contents

1

Faith, Reason, and Language

To say that the past century and a half has been a period
of enormous change in the world of Christian thought is
to state a commonplace. So great has been the change,
and so great also has been the alteration in the attitude
which Christian believers take toward change, that it is
difficult, if not utterly impossible, for most modern men
and women to think themselves back into a period in
which their faith was seen by the majority of believers as
a fixed entity, and in which the idea of movement or
growth was entertained by only a few thinkers whose insight was far in advance of the general and accepted
pattern of Christian theology in their time. Whatever we
may think of John Henry Newman, it is for most of us
today very easy to accept his dictum that "in another world
it may be otherwise, but in this world to live is to change"
—even if we are not quite certain about the conclusion
of the sentence, "and to be perfect is to have changed

often." Yet in his own day, such an idea came very much as an unwelcome shock.

The *fact* of theological development is taken for granted by all of us today. But the extent of the change, and the details of the changes which have taken place since General Theological Seminary was founded in 1817, may not be quite so obvious. We still have with us, in almost every Christian denomination, those who are resistant to the *idea* of development, even though they must accept the fact as a given reality. Certainly, there are among us many who would seek to minimize even the developments which, as a matter of fact, have taken place. But consider the topics which I propose to discuss in these lectures: the relation of faith, reason, and language; the significance of scientific thought for Christian theology; the nature of revelation and the evaluation of Jesus Christ as the disclosure of God and of man in their proper natures; the meaning and place of the Christian Church and its tradition; and the relationship of what have come to be called "the sacred" and "the secular." A moment's thought will make plain to us that in every one of these areas, our attitude today is vastly different from that taken by our fathers in the faith in the first quarter of the last century. Of course, there are abiding Christian convictions, persisting points of emphasis, along with the recurrence of questions which even in their day were being raised; nobody would wish to deny this. What I am trying to make clear is that not only do we have different ways of saying what we have to say about all these matters, but also that the things which we wish to say about them have a different quality and often a different content from what our fathers would have said. We must recognize and accept this, although some—perhaps many—are not much enamored of the difference in quality and content or of the difference in approach.

It is obvious that in a series of lectures such as these —six relatively popular lectures which are being delivered to an audience of laymen as well as theologians and which do not pretend to be exhaustive or definitive accounts of historical development or detailed theological commentary on that development—I can at best do an exploratory job. What I shall be saying will be suggestive, maybe even provocative; certainly it will be the view of one man, who is himself committed to the newer sort of approach and the newer kind of understanding of the quality and content of our Christian faith. I shall follow, in each case, a simple and obvious line, although not always according to the same pattern—different topics will suggest varying patterns. I shall try to state the way in which, 150 years ago, the generality of Christian thinkers and teachers would have looked at the matter. I shall speak of some of the important influences which have been brought to bear upon it, influences which have been responsible for modifications and alterations, or what I like to call the "reconception," of Christian thought in respect to the matter in hand. Finally, I shall offer, for what it may be worth, my own conviction as to the best way in which, in this particular era of Christian discipleship, we may understand what is being said. Quite likely I shall do less than justice to some of the older positions, not because I lack sympathy with many of them, but because in the time at my disposal it is simply impossible to present fully every aspect in each position. But my aim is a constructive one; perhaps I can best express it by saying that I am entirely sure of what

we might call the basic continuities of Christian faith—
and, indeed, of Christian theology—although at the same
time I sympathize with the dictum of Vincent of Lerins
concerning the necessity for speaking *nove* as well as *non
nova*. Unfortunately, he hardly could recognize that to do
this, to speak "in a new way," means that often we must
very seriously modify the old things about which we are
speaking, and hence must speak "new things." For as
James Russell Lowell told us, in hackneyed lines,

> New occasions teach new duties,
> Time makes ancient good uncouth.

Surely a Christian should not find *that* a disturbing
thought, since the God in whom we believe is One who
"makes all things new." He is also One who brings new
things to pass as he energizes ceaselessly in the creation
toward the accomplishment of his will in the sharing of
love.

I remember that many years ago I attended an Easter
afternoon children's service in a parish in this city. The
clergyman who was taking the service made the mistake of
asking, during his brief address, what quite obviously he
intended as a purely rhetorical question: "Need a Christian
ever be afraid?" To his consternation, a small but clear
reply came from the front row: "I should say not!" The
clergyman ended his talk very quickly; he had not quite
expected such childlike, although surely not childish, an-
ticipation of the point which, presumably, he intended to
go on to make. As we think of the changes in Christian
thought which have taken place in the years since 1817,
and know perfectly well that a great many more changes

will be taking place in the not too distant future—and that this will go on for as long as Christian faith exists in this world—we have no need to be afraid. For the God who is manifested in his action in Jesus of Nazareth is the God who has worked hitherto and even now works, who will continue working in the years to come, who is none other than the living God who in nature and in history is working out his unfailing purpose of good. We know what he *is* from what he *does*; this the Bible as a whole clearly teaches us. And one of the things he *does* is to upset, disturb, unsettle, trouble men's minds as he leads them more and more deeply into truth about himself and about their world. Hence, we know from what he does that in his innermost nature he is a God not of static truth, but of dynamic truth; not of fixed positions, but of movement and direction; and we know that for us a grasp of his reality is not a matter of immutable statement, but of growing understanding. We need never be afraid.

And now we turn to the first of our topics: faith and reason.

In theological circles 150 years ago, it was assumed without much question that the language which was used to make statements about God and his relationship with his world was a language which had meaning even if there were many persons who for one reason or another rejected that meaning. Of course, there were theologians like Renn Dickson Hampden, who in his Bampton Lectures for 1862 (published under the title *The Scholastic Philosophy, Considered in Its Relations to Christian Theology*) had questioned the validity of much of the specific terminology which had become conventional in theological circles, and had appealed for a return to more scriptural ways of making theological statements. But it would not have occurred to Hampden or any other theologian, orthodox or liberal, that the whole content of religious and theological language could be dismissed as a fiction or even called into serious question because it possessed no meaning beyond the emotive or the volitional. A problem which in our own day has become a major concern for theologians was not even on the horizon in that time.

This is not to say that the problem of religious language, and *a fortiori* of theological language, is an entirely modern problem. As long ago as Origen, Christian thinkers concerned themselves with the sort of meaning which could be given the language of Scripture; and both St. Augustine and St. Thomas Aquinas, to name but two in the history of Christian thought, discussed at length the kinds of signification which religious and theological words may be given. The doctrine of analogy and the insistence that theological statements must be predicated analogically are a testimony to an awareness of the difficulty finite men must face in speaking about God. Whether we settle for the simple analogy of likeness, or find ourselves compelled to make distinctions, such as the Scholastics employed, between analogy of appropriation, analogy of proportion, and analogy of proportionality, we are all obliged to recognize that words derived from, and initially applied to, the experiences of human finite existence can be used in reference to God only when and if we make allowance for enormous qualification and the most careful refinement in our manner of predication. But the modern problem—does religious and theological language have *any* meaning?—was certainly not a problem with which the founders of this seminary, or the theologians of their time, or, for that matter, theologians of the next hundred years, concerned themselves in any large way.

It is necessary for *us*, however, to consider this problem; and we can best look at it by setting it in the context of the continuing task of communicating the Christian faith to the men and women of any given time, and especially the task of defending the faith against those who at such times constitute what Schleiermacher called its "cultured despisers."

During the past two thousand years, Christian faith has faced many opponents, from early Gnosticism, which denied the reality of the material world, to modern materialism, which denies the existence of anything *but* the material world. In order to meet this opposition, from whatever quarter it may come, a special department in the theological disciplines has been developed; it is called *apologetics*, a technical word which does not mean what its modern cognates might suggest. Apologetics, in the theological world, means the effort both to find ways in which Christian faith may be commended to a given age and also to defend that faith against the various intellectual attacks that in each age are made upon it.

Some modern theologians, such as Karl Barth, have condemned the whole apologetic enterprise as an expression of man's faithlessness; God's word, they say, does not need any such defense and the faith is not to be commended in any peculiar fashion for each particular age— if it were, there would be the danger that the faith would be cut to the pattern of that age. Most Christians have not agreed with this attitude, however; and Anglicanism in particular has always had a large place in its thought for precisely this kind of concern for the world to which, at any given time, the gospel is to be preached.

In our own day, as we have seen, one of the most difficult problems for Christian faith is posed by the claim that religious and theological language are essentially meaningless. The most vigorous exponents of this claim belong to the movement in philosophy which goes by the name of linguistic analysis or linguistic philosophy. This movement is a reaction from what has often been styled the fuzziness of much nineteenth-century philosophy, especially in the idealist schools; it has at its heart a desire to "clean up" the use of language, to be sure that we know what we are talking about when we make statements of any sort, and to guarantee that appropriate referents are available to verify whatever statements we do make. The linguistic school is very powerful in North America today; it is also exerting considerable influence in Australia, as I learned on a visit there a few years ago. In Britain it was dominant until very recently, but now a modification is taking place, and much more room is being left for other types of philosophical inquiry, while the linguistic philosophers themselves seem more concerned with how words are *used* than with their truth-value. On the continent of Europe, where the movement originated (largely through the influence of the famous Vienna Circle), it is by no means the prevailing school of thought at the present time; indeed, it seems to have very little influence and few adherents.

An early form of linguistic thought was definitely positivistic. That is to say, it claimed that there were only two kinds of statements which one might legitimately say possessed truth-value. One kind was tautological statement, as in mathematics, where the conclusions are contained implicitly in the premises. The other kind was the type of statement which could be experimentally (by which was commonly meant "scientifically") verified. Ethical and aesthetic statements could not be proved in this way, of course; hence, they were thought to be emotive in quality. To say that an action was "bad" meant only that the speaker disliked that action. Metaphysical and theological statements were even more obviously "nonsense." By this term the positivists meant that such statements plainly had no meaning, because there was in the public domain of experience no verifiable referent to which they pointed and by which they could be checked for their truth or falsehood.

In recent years, the positivist type of linguistic philosophy has been losing its influence; even A. J. Ayer, who was its most noted British exponent, has changed his attitude and has admitted that the restriction of truth to such verifiable propositions is itself a "metaphysical" assumption, which therefore opens the door to *other* possible "metaphysical" ideas, even though he dislikes "metaphysics" and himself tries to eschew, so far as he can, propositions which have a "metaphysical" quality.

Nonetheless, the problem of religious language remains for us; and so also does the fact that large numbers of our contemporaries, unlike the contemporaries of theologians 150 years ago, are being exposed to the impact of a philosophy which insists upon *some kind* of verification of religious statements. This is not the place to discuss in any detail all the questions that are raised for us by the problem of religious language. But I can make a few suggestions which may be useful to those who are confronted today, as our ancestors were not, with some variety of linguistic philosophy but who yet wish to maintain their Christian faith as an intellectually respectable way of thinking and believing. I shall offer these suggestions *seriatim*.

(1) It is clear that certain kinds of language are appropriate for scientific inquiry and for scientific reporting, but cannot properly be employed for the understanding and description of other, and perhaps more profound, experiences. I cannot state, in terms of precise scientific verifiability, what I experience when I hear Bach's B Minor Mass, or how I feel when I see a glorious sunset at sea, or the release from self which I know when I give myself in love to another person. Neither can such language adequately account for, much less be thought to render meaningless, the persistent sense of communion with God, deliverance from sin, and newness of life in Jesus Christ, of which Christians wish to speak because they have, as they would insist, known a reality which these words point toward and in some sense describe.

(2) This does not mean that these experiences are invalid; it simply means that they are of a kind that inevitably escapes a particular sort of mesh which is useful in physics or chemistry or biology or other scientific areas. That this is the case is easily demonstrated by the fact that the linguistic thinker himself, in his nonanalytical moments, acts *practically* as if his technique were irrelevant to his loving, his appreciation of beauty, his delight in great music, his loyalty to his friends, his concern for intellectual integrity, and the like.

(3) Every man is bound to make assertions, whether explicit or implicit, which are "metaphysical" in quality.

We may dislike the word, but we are unable to avoid the fact. We cannot escape the necessity of assuming that the world is good or bad or indifferent; that it is on the side of decency or of evil; that it has or does not have a purpose. We may say that such questions are irrelevant or unnecessary; but we must, as men living in the real world, act on the assumption that some of them are true. In this sense, Pascal's assertion that "everybody must gamble" is entirely correct; and the emphasis here falls on the *must*.

(4) There is no way to *prove* by rigorous logic that one metaphysical position or another is true, although there may be a great deal which points this way or that. But it is absurd to say that man cannot properly engage in thought of this kind, for as a matter of plain fact, man has engaged in it and man does engage in it; and the greatest minds of our race, from Plato and Aristotle (and before them, too) to our own day, have been concerned with precisely such large-scale problems.

(5) Like metaphysics, religious faith is not *demonstrably* true; but, then, nobody ever thought that it was, for had they done so, they would not have called it "faith." Faith is commitment to that which grasps us; it is surrender of oneself to another—in the case of Christian faith, utter trust in God believed to be active for our wholeness in Jesus Christ. The situations in which this commitment is seen have been well described by Bishop Ian Ramsey of Durham as including both commitment *and* discernment; in the experience of surrender, the believer is made aware of some insight into the significance of that to which he surrenders and, in consequence, experiences both an enhancement of life and a deepening of his own understanding.

(6) The language in which this faith is expressed is not scientific language; it does not admit of the kind of verification appropriate to statements about the nature of energy, the structure of a cell, or the constituents of a chemical compound. Religious language—and here we recall the traditional insistence on its analogical nature—is always what I should call metaphorical language; or, as one might say, it is the language of poetry. But we need to remember that poetry is not a pretty lie; it is the consequence of a profound insight into truth, so profound that for the poet only imaginative phrases can properly describe it and effectively evoke in others an apprehension of the truth which is being stated. The language of religion as poetry is essentially the language of worship—of adoration, of confession, of grateful acceptance, of prayer in its widest sense.

(7) On the other hand, when the religious man attempts to relate his faith to other areas of his life and experience, he moves necessarily from the language of worship, which is poetic, toward the language of idea, which is conceptual; he talks of metaphysics, in short. Yet his use of this language is never without qualification by his experience of worship. The theologian—for it is he about whom we are speaking—is *not* a scientific systematizer or the builder of some metaphysical *system*, but a reflective Christian worshiper who is seeking to state the meaning of the "religious encounter" (as it is often put today) in relationship to the whole of human life and experience. His reference is always *back* to worship, to prayer, to faithful commitment; he verifies his statements by pointing to the living reality of the Christian life. And there is something more than that to which he makes appeal; he points

to the facts in history (for the Christian, this means the Bible) which gave rise to the contemporary reality which he knows in worship, prayer, and faithful commitment.

(8) Existentialism, which is the other powerful force in philosophical (and in literary) circles today, gives enormous support to this kind of attitude. It emphasizes above all else the element of "engagement," "decision," "commitment" in every man's experience, and insists that without this subjective stance no really meaningful statements can be made about that which matters most: *what it is to be a man.*

(9) Finally, as I shall argue elsewhere in these lectures, there is a metaphysic which, while of course it cannot be "proved," nevertheless does "save the appearances" —helps us to understand empirical data, religious and otherwise. Furthermore it can outargue the linguistic thinkers, can use the insights of existentialism, and can do much to authenticate the truth-value of the deliverances of faith. I am referring to the metaphysic which thinkers such as Whitehead and Hartshorne have developed and which is now commonly called process philosophy. Here is a philosophy which accepts all that can properly be said for the validity of the scientific enterprise, but rejects entirely what Prof. H. J. Paton has called the linguistic veto; it insists that the artist, the poet, the lover, and the believer have their right to be heard. Above all, here is a philosophy which sees the whole world, in all its grades and levels, as an ongoing process of such a dynamic and living quality that the restrictions imposed by any merely scientific verification are seen to be pathetically inadequate.

In the long run, I think, linguistic analysis and the philosophy associated with it will have done us a service.

They will have required us to be careful and discriminating in the use of words, to avoid flights of rhetoric which have no meaning at all (precise or otherwise), and to think carefully and accurately in all of our attempts to understand our experience and the world. But they will not rule out of court, because no type of analysis and no philosophical presuppositions ever can do that, the reality of man's religious life or destroy for him the possibility of making statements, humble and reverent as they must always be, which convey genuine meaning, not only in and to the specifically religious community, but also in the public domain of human experience and reflection.

It must be granted, I believe, that the reality of the religious life cannot be denied; it must also be granted that, with whatever qualifications and safeguards are necessary, we can speak meaningfully of that life and speak with intentional reference to God himself in the assurance that statements which are made about him in relation to his world and to men have a genuinely cognitive quality. What, then, can we say about the larger question of the way in which faith and reason are related? I believe that with a few notable exceptions, one of which will receive attention in a later lecture, Anglican theology has shown a remarkable consistency in its attitude to this question— an attitude with which I entirely agree.

On the one hand, Anglican theology has rejected that kind of supreme confidence in human reason which in some parts of the Christian world has led to the notion that the existence of God and many of his attributes can be demonstrated by logical procedures, so that any right-thinking man must needs accept these, whether he likes them or not. The position enunciated at the First Vatican

Council, that the existence of God can be demonstrated by human reason, has not been generally accepted by Anglican theologians; and even the modifications of that position made by some modern Thomists have had little appeal. On the other hand, Anglican theologians, on the whole, have not been attracted to the fideism which would deny *any* competence to the human reason in matters of ultimate concern and would insist that by revelation, and by revelation alone, do we know anything about God, our faith being either a working of God's Holy Spirit in us, with no human contribution to the matter, or a response to a revelatory statement or action proposed for our acceptance. In other words, Anglican divinity has been consistent in its unwillingness to allow that human reason in and of itself is able to establish the object of faith, or to accept the claim made by many Continental theologians in the past hundred years that faith, and faith alone, will furnish us with the requisite knowledge that God is and what God is.

When William Temple made his often-quoted remark that Anglicanism did not have any "standard" theologian but that it did have Plato, he was saying, in effect, that Anglican theology has always been prepared to associate the faith by which we live, and the statement of that faith in theological language, with the total philosophical enterprise in which human reason is necessarily the only available instrument. Certainly not all Anglican thinkers have been Platonists, although perhaps the majority of them have had a Platonizing tinge; but whoever may have been their favorite philosopher and whatever the particular mode of philosophizing to which they gave allegiance, they have been aware of, indebted to, and ready to use human reason and to regard its chastened deliverances as valuable in the theological work in which they were engaged. It was Dean Inge, I think, who once defined faith as "reason grown courageous"; and by and large, Anglican divines have talked in this kind of way. We can say that during our period of 150 years this has been quite plain. From Newman in his Anglican days (and afterward, too, as *The Grammar of Assent* plainly demonstrates), through the later Tractarian divines like Charles Gore and his disciples of the "liberal Catholic" persuasion, along with the Broad Churchmen of the nineteenth century, who in this respect were like their fellow churchmen, there has been no denigration of reason.

Frederick Denison Maurice is a supreme example of Anglican theology's attitude. Like more recent divines, such as Quick and Hodgson, Temple and Inge, Rashdall and Bethune-Baker, he saw faith and reason as friends, not enemies. All those I have mentioned have tended to say that the arguments of reason, the "ways to God" propounded by thoughtful philosophical writers, the implications which may be drawn from man's experience as a thinking, willing, and loving being, are not inconsistent with or contradicted by what faith discovers. When, in commitment to God as he is presented in the scriptural record, the possibility is given of a more or less direct acquaintance with deity, this does not deny *in toto* the enterprise by which deity is declared to be at the very least a probable, if not a necessary, inference. The Scots parson who is said to have opened his pastoral prayer with the words "Oh Thou who art our everlasting refuge and our ultimate metaphysical hypothesis" was very likely a Presbyterian; but in this prayer he spoke like an Anglican, although doubtless an Anglican would not be happy with his liturgical style.

It is no accident, therefore, that Anglican theology during our period has been criticized from the older Roman side as being too fideistic and from the modern Continental Protestant side as being too rationalistic. The fact is that Anglicanism has simply denied the supposed dichotomy. This suggests, on the one hand, that Anglicanism, by and large, has been unwilling to take the view of man which would find that in certain areas, at least, he is not at all affected by sin—that in his reason, if not in his loving and willing, he is able to proceed without prejudice and self-assertion. It also suggests, on the other hand, that Anglicanism has been unwilling to regard man as being so deeply sunk in sin that *nothing* in his activity, be it his reasoning, his willing, or his loving, is in any sense whatsoever to be trusted. In our own time this Anglican "middle path" has led to the charge, once again made in many quarters, that Anglican divinity is essentially Pelagian. Nobody worth bothering about these days is prepared to take the extreme, old-fashioned, rationalistic view of man's capacity to reach truth with undeviating accuracy, but on all sides we are told that man is a grievous sinner who is infallibly (if that is the right adverb) in error and whose reason is the chief seat of his proud and arrogant claim to be lord of the universe. This charge against Anglican theology can be borne with equanimity, I think. It is not in accordance with the facts, and those who make it are themselves caught in the peculiar situation of being obliged to use their reason to deride their reason.

However that may be, most Anglicans in the last 150 years would gladly have accepted the celebrated remark of

the Cambridge Platonist, drawn in fact from Scripture itself, that man's reason is "the candle of the Lord." They
would not have ventured to say that it is *more* than a
"candle"; they would have acknowledged gladly that man's
reason is not in itself "the Light of the World." But they
would have insisted that when we have a candle, we can
see *something* in the darkness, although we must also rejoice that "the Dayspring from on high" has visited us. In
other words, they were willing to put some trust in the
human reason. And they have been able to do this because
they have learned, from the Cambridge divines to whom
I have just referred, from Coleridge and Maurice, and from
many another in their history, that the use of the human
reason is not merely a ratiocinative and syllogistic exercise,
but is also what the ancient Fathers of the Church believed
it to be: a participation, however partial and dim, in the
reason who is the Logos of the world, who is indeed *God's*
Word. We men are sinners, yes; but despite our sin, we are
still God's creatures, made in his image—and the image of
God dwelling in all men and working through them all, is
God the Word "by whom all things were made," "who is
the light that lighteneth every man," and who in one Man,
Jesus Christ our Lord, "was made flesh and dwelt among
us, full of grace and truth."

2

Christian Faith and Scientific Thought

We are concerned in this chapter with the modern scientific description of the universe and of man, and with the position that the Christian religion can hold in such a world. We shall first of all consider the scientific situation; then the more general philosophical point of view which may be drawn from scientific study; and finally, the position of Christian faith in the sort of world these two present.

A survey of current scientific thought must necessarily be brief. There is no time in this lecture to outline in any detail the many new developments in this field, even if I were competent to make the attempt. Yet a few important facts, taken more or less at random from the several sciences, will be helpful in giving us a general line of approach.

On the large-scale view, this planet seems relatively unimportant in the physical scheme of things. The distance of the earth from the sun is 93,000,000 miles and the mass of the sun is 330,000 times that of the earth, while its diameter is 864,000 miles; our earth's diameter is 4,000 miles. The star nearest to us is 275,000 times as far as our sun, or 4.3 light-years; and the giant Betelgeuse, with a diameter 300 times that of our sun, is 210 light-years away. Man's *physical* insignificance in this scheme is quite plain. On the other hand, physics has now demonstrated that the substratum of the world is made up of electrical charges, the exact nature of which is quite uncertain, whose activity is sufficiently indeterminate, on the small scale, to introduce an element of what has been called super-controlled chance into the very heart of things. Certainly the principle of indeterminacy, if it is in fact true, does not establish freedom of the will; but we have here a reversal of the strict deterministic position necessitated by the classical Newtonian physics. Furthermore, the universe would appear to be finite; and space is said by most experts to be curved, so that (as one writer has put it) the nearest star may be only the other side of the farthest star. This and other consequences of relativity physics have turned older ideas of the physical world upside down.

The application of the theory of development originally drawn from biological study has been extended into the physical sphere; and we have been shown a cosmic workshop in which universes and their member planets are made and unmade, apparently with terrific violence. And the ultimate constituents of these universes are infinitesimal electrical charges, evidently more or less unpredictable in their individual movement or variation. From one of the giant universe collisions, our own world may date its appearance. In the biological realm, this same general theory of change, today accepted by every competent authority, shows a processive movement in organic life, with ordered development from the first protoplasm up to what are now said to be more than 250,000 species of invertebrate animals and some 25,000 species of vertebrate animals. There has been a gradual advance, proceeding over millions of years, both in integration and in differentiation, toward the emergence of ever-higher (in the sense of more differentiated, yet more integrated) forms of life. A continuous process of change has been taking place, moving along the line of development toward the appearance of conscious and self-conscious personality and bringing into explicit expression qualities implicit in the original stock.

In another direction, psychology has altered our notion of man's emotional, volitional, and intellectual activity. The existence today of behavioristic, dynamic, psychoanalytic, and Gestalt schools, each with its own theories and principles, is indicative of some confusion in this particular field; but it is probable that a unified psychological scheme will be found within a relatively short time. In the meanwhile, it is clear that the present tendency is to assert that the mental life of the higher animals, and *a fortiori* of man, is part of an organic whole which includes mechanical stimulus-reaction chains as well as the more or less deterministic realm of the subconscious, but yet in itself is more than these and is capable of using them in a manner which roughly may be called purposive. Furthermore, the study of living, conscious matter at the physiological level has demonstrated what it is now fashionable to call the psychosomatic nature of such organisms as man.

Finally, anthropology and sociology have altered our conception of man's history; and we know more of the primitive origins of his social, aesthetic, religious, and even his scientific ideas, and see something of the principles which have governed their growth. The perspective on man has altered tremendously; he is now placed in a long line of development, both in body and in mind, and is seen against the background of a natural world of which he is, in some quite real and definite sense, a constituent part.

But despite this startling expansion of the scientific outlook in recent years, all of us are aware that at the same time a profound change has come over scientific theorizing since the halcyon days of the great naturalists of the last century. We can have some sympathy with the fear that Christian thinkers felt, during much of the last 150 years, that scientific study would *destroy* all faith; yet theirs was really a faithless fear, and we may be glad that Newman and Kingsley, to name but two, did not share it. In any event, no longer do scientists hold with certainty that their studies will eventually enable them to give an exhaustive account of the entire world in purely mechanical terms. They are quite aware that there are more things in the world than science can account for, although they are as insistent as ever upon the necessity of pushing the mechanistic explanation as far as it will go.

Art, poetry, friendship, truth, moral standards, religious experience—all of these, in the last analysis, elude the scientific experimentalist, although undoubtedly science has something to say about each one of them. In the final reckoning they are *sui generis;* they cannot be explained by strict science, since they do not fall within the area of that which is susceptible of measurement, dissection, or mathematical statement in terms of equations. We need not agree with all that has been said in recent books on the subject to see the importance of the disinterested admission that science is not the whole story, and that other realms of human experience have their genuine contribution to make to our understanding of ourselves and of this world in which our lives are set. With all their epistemological vagaries, such as (for example) the tendency of some physicists to succumb to idealist views of knowing, recent writing has shown a widespread revolt, among scientists themselves, against a purely naturalistic explanation of the universe.

To a large degree, this has been the result of an astonishing change in the accepted conception of the nature and function of science itself. Distinguished French writers on scientific theory, such as Meyerson, Poincaré, Duhem, and LeRoy, were among the first to insist that so-called scientific laws may not properly be regarded as rigid cast-iron definitions, deterministic in nature and by necessity demanding the mechanistic outlook which would see the world as a vast, mindless machine. The French theorists, who were later joined by many English and German scientists and philosophers of science, affirmed, on the contrary, that the laws of science are in reality more like convenient working hypotheses, or summary statements of statistical averages, or a series of observed sequences; these are indispensable in the furtherance of research, but they must remain open to qualification and probable correction in the light of new data obtained by fresh and more precise experiment or observation; and they must undergo continual expansion and development.

In a contribution to a discussion of the nature of science conducted several years ago in a French periodical —I am ashamed to say that I cannot now locate the reference—Émile Picard stated that for many modern scientists, theories follow one another with a rapidity that is sometimes alarming, and they take on an increasingly schematic and symbolic coloring. Picard went on to point out that the history of the sciences is full of failures; theories, like books, have had their day. Hence, the conception of natural law has changed amazingly in the past fifty years. For example, he points out, the quantum theory has come to modify our ideas on continuity, while the calculus is taking an important part in physics, so that the so-called laws of nature appear as no more than probable and have lost the rigidity which they had for our predecessors. Those who make a fetish of science can be left to their dogmatism. Science, as Montaigne said, is a fine adornment of the mind and a wonderfully useful implement; but it is essential that we realize its limitations and do not permit ourselves to be deceived about what we can expect from it. So much for Picard.

It should be realized, however, that this general recognition of the limits of science does not in any sense invalidate the use (where this is possible) of mechanistic concepts and methods in scientific investigation, nor does it invalidate the insistence that such mechanistic procedures must be pressed to the utmost. What it does make clear is that while the extent of mechanism in the universe is quite certainly much larger than we might have anticipated, it is also true that it is *relatively* unimportant. This was said long ago by Lotze; and its truth is being realized anew today. Science gives us, at least in part, a mechanistic view of the world, but the mechanistic view does not go all the way. Measurement, analysis, classification, genetic studies, and the rest of scientific procedure are of vast importance; but they do not exhaust the experience of man.

We may say, then, that many contemporary scientists believe, and indeed proclaim, that in the long view of man's experience and of the universe as a whole, we need not only the findings of science, but also synthesis, the faculty of appreciation, and the data discovered and known in realms other than the scientific. Scientific investigation has immeasurably increased our conception of the size and age of our world; the new vistas are breathtaking, the reach vaster than our mind can grasp. Science has taught us our animal descent, has traced our racial history, has shown us the origins of our institutions and customs, has found strange new areas in our mental and emotional life, has discovered an incalculable mass of fact which within limits contributes to our understanding of ourselves and our world. All this must find its place in any complete outlook on man and the world. On the other hand, science has discovered for itself that it cannot solve the riddle of the universe, and least of all can it produce the fruit of the Spirit or provide motives for unselfish endeavor.

This change in scientific outlook has been followed in some quarters by a profound skepticism. The human mind can no longer be trusted, it is said. Science, which was thought to give us universal truth, is now seen to be a "false messiah," and its findings are as much wishful thinking as anything else in human experience. Science has been shown up as an imposter. Still other modern thinkers have taken refuge in irrational divisions of human experience; they have denied that there is any principle of unity in our knowledge, and have said that the disjointed (and to them contradictory) results of science, art, morality, and perhaps even religion must all be taken as equally true or false, as our preferences may incline us or as pragmatic considerations may impel us.

But surely we cannot rest in either position. Is there not good reason for trusting, however reservedly, the human mind and its rational powers? Admittedly they cannot give us *all* the truth, but do they not give us some partial and real truth? How can we operate scientifically, or even pragmatically, without presupposing some principle of unity which sees the world and all things in it as being of a piece, as open to our quest, and as in some sense validly known by us? The skeptical or the dualistic tendency in some exponents of scientific thought may well lead to intellectual suicide; here science needs new faith in itself and its methods.

Most working scientists do not share these needlessly extreme views. They do not hesitate to affirm that science has discovered real truth which is complementary to, not contradictory of, the findings in other departments of human experience and thought. Many of them, indeed, concur with religious faith in declaring that in man's mental, aesthetic, and moral life, and in his spiritual aspirations, we have our profoundest insight into the nature of reality. Science, religion, and other avenues of approach to that reality are all valid in their way, and will in the end be found to fit into one total scheme.

We now turn to some observations on the general question of the relation of religion and science, which so exercised our fathers in the faith during the last century. "God" cannot be proved from science: all that science could show would be a creative power or cosmic force, working, perhaps, toward an end conceived to be good. But despite man's physical insignificance in the scheme of things, he has a central place in our understanding of the world—that is, as soon as what may loosely be called the qualitative or, in Whitehead's term, "aesthetic" aspect of experience is given its proper recognition. In this way the new scientists, as I believe Dr. F. R. Tennant once suggested, have in fact reinstated man in something like the position which he held before the Copernican revolution. Since it is man who has discovered all the important scientific data about the physical universe, it is impossible to regard him merely as an animal or a machine; his insight, intuition, inferences, impressions, and apprehensions are valuable for, and indeed central to, our understanding of the world.

If science cannot give a complete account of man and of the world, there is room (as I have insisted) for other avenues of approach, notably the religious. We do not need to wait for some distinguished scientist to tell us that we may believe in God; science itself could not proceed without its own kind of faith in reality and in truth, which amounts to an implicit faith in what religion explicitly calls God. Yet it has been an important aid to religion to have famous scientists confess that apart from religious faith and experience they can see no solution to the problem of the world and its meaning. Modern scientists are very much humbler than were many of their predecessors in the nineteenth and early twentieth centuries. As Dr. A. C. Bouquet has pointed out, modern science generally has nothing to say against, and may even be thought to have much to say for, the self-existent, self-expressive Reality whom faith calls God.

But religious faith, for its part, has no right whatever to deny the fullest scientific investigation of all data, nor can it attempt to force antiquated science on its believers. For example, within the world which scientists study—that is, the whole field of phenomena—miracle, in the sense of sudden intrusion from outside into the ordered operation of the physical universe, is an inadmissible hypothesis. This may seem to be an a priori judgment; but it is essential to the scientist, who would assert that while we know nothing about "laws" which never may be broken, we do know a great deal about regularities which as a matter of observed fact never are broken. The scientist is here making no denial of new truth, new facts, or unexpected data; he is insisting on the orderliness which he has discovered everywhere and which alone makes consistent study possible. And even from the point of view of religion, it may be said that a Christian faith which rests solely upon arbitrary interventions into a world which otherwise gets on nicely without the assistance of the deity can never endure, for it is a faith which is ultimately faithless—it fails to see God as the continually sustaining Reality which the deepest insight of the Old Testament so plainly indicates.

On the other hand, science has nothing to say against the view of the "supernatural" held by Baron von Hügel and many other contemporary religious writers, who regard it (in Dr. A. H. Dakin's words) as "the rational and spiritual values and realities inherent in the structure of nature," and also as God himself, "not only in his immanence but also in his transcendence." But God is not to be sought in the gaps of our knowledge, in those places where we do not yet understand the causal nexus; nor is he to be found only in what are taken as sudden intrusions into an ordered world. There are vast differences, and unprecedented and unpredictable emergences and changes, in the process of evolution; but these are always, in the end, found to be related to and congruous with the generally pervasive line of activity, occurring within a greater continuity as part of the operation of the Reality in and behind the whole grand order, once this is seen with full recognition of its heights, depths, and varied levels.

But, it may be asked, does not psychological investigation show that religious experience, and *a fortiori* religion itself, is mere illusion? In answer, it must be pointed out that such investigation has nothing whatever to say about the question of the *validity* of such experience. Science generally is not concerned with such ultimate questions; and the psychologists who deny the transsubjective reference of religious experience, in the widest sense of that term, do so on the basis of their own naturalistic philosophy, and not as a result of strictly scientific study. In the mid-1930's, Prof. C. C. J. Webb, in his *Religion and Theism*, brilliantly showed, once and for all, that the effort to account for this experience without invoking some more than human Reality is certain to fail. Not only is it unable to account for the note of ultimacy in the experience, hence destroying the characteristic quality of the matter under investigation, but it also deposes scientific experience itself, since, on precisely the same grounds and following exactly the same procedure, that experience also can be shown to be illusory. The conclusion of the more sober psychologist may be put by saying that on the one hand, religious experience is not "miraculous" in the unacceptable sense of a strange, unrelated intervention into purely human experience, and on the other hand, is not an illusion. It is open for interpretation as a penetration of the finite by that which brought the finite into being. Religious experience is a point at which there may be a unique release of transhuman energy into human affairs; and it may be this which explains its stupendous results in the lives of men.

Religion, if it minds its own business, has nothing to

fear from science; nor has science, when it also minds its own business, anything to fear from religion. Science acts as a purifying agent, cleansing away outworn mythological ideas and the mistaken views of the world which have accumulated about religious faith; it can make faith stronger and more significant for men. As Dr. W. W. Manross, one-time tutor here, remarked in a valuable essay published in the 1934 *Seminarian,* a booklet which used to appear in this seminary each year, there is "a growing recognition that the scientific method, however important its contribution to human knowledge, cannot, because of its essentially empirical character, provide that unified view of human life and human aims which is essential to worthy living." Yet it must always be remembered that science is not merely a valuable method of study and an important aid in practical affairs; it is also, to quote again from Dr. Manross, "a deeply religious form of asceticism," because of its "rigorous subjection of the investigator's wishes to the demands of reason and carefully observed experience."

Let us now turn to the philosophy of science or, rather, to the philosophy which modern science seems to suggest. There are many types of systems offered today in the name of modern thought, and they are vastly different from each other. I have already discussed linguistic philosophy and have referred to existentialism. But it is fair to say that there is another significant trend in modern philosophy, a trend which is quite generally accepted even though it is most explicitly stated by certain writers whom I shall mention. In recent works of popular philosophy, for example, while the given author may seem to differ quite considerably from other modern thinkers, yet usually if he is concerned with metaphysical matters, his orientation is in the main that which I shall be describing. It cannot be said of modern philosophy, once we have got beyond linguistic analysis and existentialist description, that there are only very diverse individual opinions. In fact, there is today a dominant philosophical orientation toward the world, which may aptly be described as (*a*) evolutionary, (*b*) emergent, and (*c*) organistic or holistic. I shall comment on each of these points.

First, the modern thinker sees the world as process or dynamic movement. He may not regard this as an exhaustive statement, but he accepts the fact. For the first time in the history of human thought, laymen and philosophers have no choice but to understand the universe and everything in it, not as a collection or system of *things*, but as a continuous series of activities. This profound alteration in our thinking is comparatively recent. Adumbrations of evolutionary philosophy were known before 1859, when Charles Darwin published *The Origin of Species*; Heraclitus understood the world as flux, and even St. Augustine has statements about development in the natural world. But it was from Darwin's work, and the subsequent application of the biological theory of evolution to other areas, that the new outlook achieved general acceptance. Christian theologians at first did not like it; now none reject it. We all assume that we live in a world where change has been going on for untold millions of years, both in the physical structure of things long before life came and after that in the appearance of new species; we all realize the constant movement, the processive quality, which characterizes the world and everything in it.

The second factor is a strong emphasis on emergence.

By this I mean the appearance of genuinely new levels and types in the process of evolution. No longer is it maintained, as sometimes was the case in the nineteenth century, that the history of the world is simply the story of the automatic rearrangement of what was there all the time. The evolution of the universe is not the haphazard result of some "fortuitous concourse of atoms," as mechanists in that century used to say; neither is it the simple *appearance* of alteration in what is in reality a dead world of mechanical "parts." The whole processive movement is characterized by creativity; there is genuine development and growth, the appearance of real novelty. We have been led to see that along with the continuity which evolution indicates, there are also genuine and unpredictable differences. These cannot be regarded as mere resultants of the combination of constituent parts; they are quite new, both in quality and in function. Yet, so far as can be discovered, there have been no intrusions from *outside* the process. We can say that while there may have been partial anticipations of the new levels, yet conditions are such that there actually does *come* into existence this or that new level in the process. We do not know exactly what makes the change, or the precise moment when it occurs; the movement is both gradual and sudden. There the new entity is—and that is the fact to be accounted for.

In the by now hackneyed illustration, oxygen and hydrogen do not combine to produce a resultant which has no "novelty" about it and which might satisfactorily be called oxygen-plus-hydrogen, with functions and qualities that are merely additive of the prior two elements. Rather, they combine to produce a new emergent, the qualitatively different thing H_2O, which, while it is made up of two atoms of hydrogen and one of oxygen combined to make three atoms, yet is something quite other than mere oxygen-plus-hydrogen. Water cannot be explained without remainder in terms of its original chemical constituents, for it is not simply those constituents, but a *new* entity. From this union of oxygen and hydrogen has appeared, emergently—that is, as a *new* appearance—something which has its own specific characteristics. Furthermore, this new emergent indicates latent possibilities in the elements of which it is composed, but which do not in fact have these functions and qualities until the emergence occurs. Even more obviously is this the case when we consider the emergence of living matter; it is supremely true of conscious and self-conscious life, above all of human life, with its valuational, appreciative, moral, and aesthetic qualities.

This type of interpretation, when carried through the whole evolutionary process, demands a view of the world as a graded system of emergents, in which more of the underlying nature of the whole process is disclosed in the higher and more richly complex sectors than in the lower and less fully differentiated levels. The process is to be judged by its end rather than its beginning. What is the explanation of these new emergents? Why do they appear when they do? From such considerations, many contemporary philosophers have come to regard the universe as holistic, societal, or organismic. Each entity in this emergent universe is *more* than the sum of its parts; it is an organic society and can be understood only in a world which is also like that. The unity which is observed in any entity and in the whole process is a unity as a real "whole"; in Smuts's phrase, it is holistic. The whole is in each case characterized by its own specific qualities and functions, and is explicable (insofar as it is explicable at all) only in terms of its *drive*, its "subjective aim," as Whitehead called it. It moves toward a goal, whether that striving be conscious or merely the seeking of self-realization at some other level. The constituent parts of each emergent entity are taken up into the larger activity of the next "whole" which includes them; and when they are taken up into the new level, they manifest new functions which result from their sharing in the new configuration. They are organically united in a purposive manner toward the achievement of their end or object. In this manner, the conception of mechanism, although true in one sense, is subsumed in a larger and more pervasive teleology.

Thus the whole world is disclosed to us as an emergent series of organisms, some small and some great, some less and some more richly differentiated. The series starts from the abstraction of space-time, and mounts through matter (which Whitehead regarded as composed of tiny organisms or societies, such as atoms and molecules) to vegetative and animal life, then on to intelligence and personality, and to the aesthetic, with its apprehension of value. Finally, as Whitehead and Hartshorne, among others, insist, there is the level at which relationship with the inclusive, purposive Reality is possible—that is to say, the appearance of man's religious awareness. There are possible subdivisions of each of these several grades; the process is by no means neat and uniform in development; but the scheme is generally accepted as an accurate description of the way things go.

Here again there are questions. Is such a process self-explanatory? What is the basic nature of the larger teleology which seems involved in it? What does the fact of organism suggest about the meaning of the whole?

Some thinkers are content to say that there must be some unconscious *nisus* which directs the whole course of events; others, discerning the contradiction in the conception of "unconscious purpose," assert that there is in and behind it all some "stream" of consciousness; some are prepared to affirm an immanent deity whose purpose is being realized in the world. Some also still hold, but not too securely, to a rather old-fashioned naturalism, but this must be qualified as being a "dialectical materialism," in Marxist fashion, and it raises once again innumerable questions which can be answered only by a departure from that position.

By and large, however, it is realized that the evolutionary movement shows signs of following a direction, and it would be pretty generally agreed that the direction is most clearly manifested in man and his grasp of values. Successive events and levels in the process provide insight, and in their degree a permanent insight, as they reach higher grades of differentiation and integration, into the nature of the whole enterprise. History is of special significance here; in historical change there is a manifestation of something vital to the nature of the world, but it is not to be dissociated from the natural order in which it occurs. While history cannot be given an almost absolute place as being alone significant—despite Croce, the followers of his school of Neo-Hegelianism, and the philosophers of the Marxian school—yet in historical events, in historical facts, and in historical consequences, as these are seen in the lives of men, with their apprehension of value, their purposes, and their ideal strivings, there is something more than merely adventitious happening; there are actual emergents in the order of the universe, declaring something about that from which they emerge.

Physically, quantitatively, the significance of man and his history appears slight; qualitatively, man and his experience are central to our understanding of the way things go. On the physical and biological levels, man is organic to the world which produced him; and it is obvious that his ideals, his moral, aesthetic, scientific, and religious experience, are part of his very being. If he is so intimately related to the scheme of things, that scheme cannot be explained without taking him into account; neither can it be understood without attention to the events, facts, trends, and historical development which are part of human life on this planet. Human personality, with its history and with its insight into its history, may legitimately be taken to be the highest level in the cosmic process, so far as we know. As a real emergent it demands explanation, for it presupposes an environment of a sort adequate both for its own understanding and for its own expression.

In the light of these tendencies in philosophy, an epistemology of a realistic sort seems required. No longer can man's experience be cut off from the world by some ultimate dualism. He and his world are organic, his experience is a real experience, and his knowledge is the response to the impact of the world upon him. In the writings of William Temple, one of the notable philosophical theologians of this century, this important fact was emphasized; perhaps the way has been prepared for a synthesis which will place man once again at the heart of things, not physically, but as providing a clue to his world, not abstracted from reality as if he were a "sport," but organic to it and, hence, revelatory of its ongoing process.

A few remarks on individual philosophers may be helpful at this point. Henri Bergson was among the first to protest against a purely mechanistic explanation of the evolutionary process. His view of life as *élan vital,* which overcomes sheer necessity and springs forth in rich creativity in the ever-changing forms of our world, was extraordinarily valuable at the turn of the century in showing the inadequacy of nineteenth-century conceptions. Christian theologians may feel his earlier theory inadequate— and it is interesting to note that in his last work, *The Two Sources of Morality and Religion,* he finally identified the *élan vital* with the immanent action of a creative God —but his defense of creativity, freedom, and novelty was a very great service indeed.

Next there was Samuel Alexander, whose Gifford Lectures, *Space Time and Deity,* proposed an evolutionary philosophy which accepted new emergents "with natural piety," insisting on the inadequacy of the mechanistic interpretation and urging that the universe is a graded epigenetic system from space-time up to deity. Just what was for him the point of origin of the whole process is uncertain; it was not deity, for to Alexander, deity seemed always to be an ideal—the universe was pregnant with deity never quite born, as it were, a realm of ideality which attached to and beckoned the existent world on to ever-higher levels. Such a view is hardly adequate to the demands of reason and the reality of religious life; but the forward look, the freedom, and the creativity of the world as portrayed by Alexander are surely important to emphasize.

Alexander's metaphysic was taken over, but with very significant changes, by Prof. C. Lloyd-Morgan in his Gifford Lectures, *Emergent Evolution* and *Life, Mind, and*

Spirit. Here we have a graded universe of matter, life, mind, and spirit, with a conscious *nisus* which Lloyd-Morgan identified with the Divine Logos. It has often been charged that the element of divine transcendence was overlooked in his scheme, which indeed is somewhat Spinozistic in outlook; yet the Christian character of his thought was made clear when he wrote that it was his belief that the immanent Logos is uniquely self-expressed in the person of Jesus Christ. Deity was for Lloyd-Morgan operative throughout the whole grand system of nature, evoking the successive levels, self-expressed in them, and specially manifest in Christ. This noble conception is readily available for Christian use, and was employed to good effect by William Temple and by W. R. Matthews in several books dealing with the Christian concept of deity.

Mention should also be made of the work of Gen. Jan Christian Smuts, chiefly in his volume entitled *Holism and Evolution.* Here again the world was seen as an emergent process, whose explanation is in its whole-making character—the fact that it is marked by a tendency to produce ever more inclusive organisms. No transcendent explanatory principle was invoked; the universe itself was seen as a totality, a super organism whose holistic character was explained by itself. This is hardly satisfactory; and Prof. Alfred North Whitehead, whose views in many ways were similar to Smuts's, found an explanatory "principle of concretion" a necessity. This principle evokes, from the realm of unlimited ideal possibility or potentiality, that which becomes actual or concrete in the particular "events" of the world.

Whitehead was probably in his time the greatest of

philosophers, and his scheme is among the most impressive ever presented to man. This is not the place to present in detail the elements of process philosophy as Whitehead developed it. In another book, *Religious Process-Thought*, I have endeavored to do just this, with attention also to the amplification of Whitehead found in Charles Hartshorne. Neither shall I discuss the thought of Pierre Teilhard de Chardin, the French Jesuit whose posthumously published books have done so much to popularize this kind of approach to the relationship between Christian faith and scientific discovery. I content myself with urging my readers to go on, from the rather sketchy presentation which I have attempted in this lecture, to read for themselves at least three books by Whitehead—*Adventures of Ideas, Process and Reality,* and *Religion in the Making*—and two by Hartshorne—*Man's Vision of God* and *The Divine Relativity*—and then to study Charles E. Raven's Gifford Lectures, *Natural Religion and Christian Theology,* which cover most of the ground that I should like to cover if I had the time and skill to do so. Finally, I urge the reading of a non-Anglican's book, J. B. Cobb's *A Christian Natural Theology,* to introduce a specifically American contribution to the use of Whiteheadian and Hartshornean process thought for the purposes of Christian theology. I need hardly add that this type of philosophy is the one to which I personally subscribe.

Note that all the writers whom I have mentioned are sympathetic to moral, aesthetic, and religious experience. They feel that such experience gives real insight into the nature of the world; they believe that it is no mere illusion to say that there are other than scientific avenues of approach to reality. They would agree that in all of his many ways of knowledge and life, man is put into contact with some genuine reality; they differ among themselves as to the nature of that reality and its relationship to man. Probably none of the systems which I have briefly sketched is in itself completely satisfactory to the Christian theologian in giving a fully adequate account of God and his relation to the world, and especially in respect to that prior action of God in and upon his world which is the heart of the Christian's insistent faith. But Christianity must somehow be set in the context of this new world outlook. When this is done, Christianity, by reason of its own specific data, will be able to supplement modern philosophies as it has ancient ones.

Fundamentally, Christian theology must maintain the need for a transcendent principle of explanation. The immanent process described by the scientific theorists and the philosophers to whom I have referred must be seen as the operation of a Reality which is more than that process. Whitehead and Hartshorne have both seen this; hence their special appeal to some of us.

For undifferentiated immanentism and for sheer pantheism, Christian thought would substitute the panentheistic conception of a Reality operating in, yet inexhaustibly more than, all things. That Reality is the ground of change; and the evolutionary movement itself is the working out of some great purpose envisaged by that Reality. The fuller expression of the creative purpose explains the emergence of new levels in the process, each being in its degree revelatory of some aspect of the underlying activity and transcendent source. The world can never explain God; it can give us hints as to his nature and "plan." On the other hand, only a God who is himself an actual existent can offer any adequate explanation of the course of events. Immanentism does away with the fact of God as an unexhausted and distinct reality, and appears to remove all moral standards by making every level equally indicative of the divine being and purpose. Yet the sense of "the other" and "the holy," the ultimate and the sacred, and the presence of moral obligation in our daily life are patent facts in human experience. In the concept of God that Christian thought suggests, God's distinctive reality is safeguarded; ethical discrimination is preserved; the mysterious reach of human experience beyond itself is validated; and a principle of unity is secured by which meaning is given to the scientific, aesthetic, moral, and religious experience of man.

Christians are committed to the belief that their faith provides the most adequate, fertile, and rewarding interpretation of reality, of the universe, and of man. But it is not only an interpretation; it is the power to live nobly and well in the midst of this present world. The way is open for a presentation of Christian faith as man's nearest approach to God, an approach which takes men to the heart of God only because God has first deigned to draw near to men. By placing Jesus Christ, seen as the uniquely full disclosure in human terms of immanent and transcendent Reality, or God, at the center of its faith, Christianity draws stupendous conclusions about the world. From the distinctive Christian experience there emerges a distinctive view of the whole creation, for which the union of Deity and humanity effected in Christ is both focus and point of radiation. The world, on this view, is created, sustained, and penetrated by an eternal, spiritual, superpersonal, inexhaustibly rich, self-existent Reality whose nature is love. Self-disclosed by his activity throughout the creative process, he has concentrated that self-disclosure, for men on this planet, in the human life of Christ. Through that human life, a new energy has been released into the world of men which enables them to share in the divine purpose and to live in continuing communion with One who rose victorious over death and now reigns at the heart of the Reality whose intimate self-expression he is known to be. Through this new emergent, God "got into human life" in a degree entirely unparalleled and, for Christian faith, never to be surpassed, since what has once been done need not be done again.

This Christian faith must be reconceived in the light of all that we now know about ourselves and our world. We do not need a reduction or accommodation of Christianity to fit the vagaries of any given science or philosophy. But there must be a sympathetic understanding of these trends of thought, as St. Thomas Aquinas sympathetically studied Aristotelian philosophy and presented Christianity in its terms. What we most need is the daring venture of placing Christianity in a new context. In that context, we shall see once again how it fulfills its function of interpreting human experience and giving meaning to the whole of things. The Christian data have a unique importance; they are rightly held to be normative for our understanding of man, the world, and God. It is only by the task of reconception that we can maintain this faith and show that it still offers power to live richly and fruitfully, because it is the ultimate explanation of our place in this mysterious world.

3

Revelation and the Christological Question

Dean Mansel's famous Bampton Lectures of 1858, entitled *The Limits of Religious Thought*, fall neatly within the period considered in this series. In these lectures the first Waynflete Professor of Moral and Metaphysical Philosophy at the University of Oxford, who later became the Dean of St. Paul's, argued that the mind of man is utterly incompetent to acquire any knowledge of God through the exercise of its natural faculties. The *only* way to a knowledge of God is through the supernatural revelation given by God himself, a revelation whose truth is attested by the miracles which attended it and whose authority is therefore that full divine endorsement which makes it binding upon men. What Mansel may have intended to argue is one thing; what many, if not most, of his readers understood him to mean is another and is quite plain. He was taken to say that because of the radical limitation of human reason, which in effect made impossible any valid metaphysical statements, the enterprise of philosophical theology is to be rejected and the case for theism is to rest upon revelation alone. It sounds very much like the earlier Karl Barth in our own time.

The reaction to these lectures was varied, but the response of Frederick Denison Maurice was not in doubt. The year after the Bamptons were delivered, Maurice published his scathing reply under the title *What Is Revelation?* In this book, exactly the opposite position of Mansel's was defended by the then famous, if not entirely trusted, author of *The Kingdom of Christ*. Whereas Mansel had taken his departure from a position not far from philosophical agnosticism and had denigrated human reason, Maurice started from a generally Platonic philosophical view, insisting that by man's very nature he is participant in that reason or logos which in its fullness is incarnate in the person of Jesus Christ. The Johannine emphasis, always so strong in Maurice's thought, was employed to show that the main tradition of Christian theology throughout its history had been at the poles from Mansel's assertions. On the contrary, Maurice claimed, it was essential to the whole Christian position to interpret the world as a reflection, because it is the creation, of the divine Word "by whom all things were made." That same Word is also "the light that lightens every man"; hence, reason in man is indeed what St. Augustine long ago had declared it to be: a participation in the divine Word. So Maurice went on to affirm, against Mansel, that there is indeed some genuine knowledge of God in every human mind. The divine Word was enfleshed in Jesus Christ to correct, but also to complete, the knowledge of God given in the very fact of man's humanity.

Of course, Maurice did not intend to suggest that reason, in the sense of logical exercises, speculative activity, or human ratiocination, was the connecting link between God and man. By the term "reason" he meant what Coleridge had meant, and earlier than Coleridge, what the Cambridge Platonists had meant, and earlier than them, what the Alexandrine theologians and many other patristic writers had meant: the whole being of man in his outreach toward grasping the underlying significance of the creation and the God of creation. In fact, he meant very much what Paul Tillich has meant when he has distinguished between reason in its popular sense of the employment of logical methods and reason in its deeper sense as the interpretative, evaluational activity of man as he seeks to relate himself to that which is his "ultimate concern"; and Maurice emphasized the latter meaning as the significant one in theological discourse.

We should not assume that Mansel's position was the one taken by most orthodox thinkers of his time. For them —at least for theologians in the Anglican Church—the more usual view was that by means of natural theology, taking the data of experience and employing the logical categories with which they can be handled, it was possible to claim with a high degree of probability, even if not with complete certainty, that God exists, that man has a certain kind of freedom, and that a future life will ensure the correct balancing of good and evil so that justice finally will be done. In addition to this, so to say on top of this, the scriptural revelation had been given. In the sacred books, these theologians held, God had given the final, complete, and entirely adequate revelation of himself, first by inspiring the prophets of the Jewish dispensation and guiding the chosen people in their history, and then by himself entering the world in the person of Jesus Christ. In Jesus, both in his miracles and in his teaching, the last word had been spoken. And of this self-disclosure of God to men, the Bible was the inspired record—inspired in such a full sense that no error was found in it, every word having been "dictated by the Holy Spirit"—as a Roman pontiff was to phrase it not many years later.

The interesting point for us is that Mansel's position, while not typical of theologians of his own time, also is not untypical of a considerable number of defenders of orthodox Christianity in our day. These defenders have been so overwhelmed by the devastating attack of the linguistic philosophers on metaphysical and theological statement, to which I referred in an earlier lecture; they have been so impressed by the rejection, by Karl Barth and others, of the whole enterprise of natural theology in all its traditional forms; or they have been so driven by the work of biblical critics, students of comparative religion, and experts in the history of religion that they have felt themselves compelled to say that *no* deliverances of man's reason are trustworthy, *no* attempts on man's side can reach to any positive and meaningful statements about the divine reality, and, hence, knowledge of God is available *only* from that revelation of himself which is contained in Holy Scripture or (if they happen to be more catholically minded) in those assertions concerning the nature and purposes of God which are contained in the dogmatic pronouncements of the Church.

I need hardly remark that this extreme position, which has not been uncommon in our day even in some Anglican circles, is riddled with difficulties. The enormous number of questions—logical, epistemological, psychological, historical, bibliocritical—which can be asked about it should be enough to make any thoughtful person hesitate a long time before he commits himself to this view. What is important, however, is that we reflect upon the great change which for most of us has taken place in our own thinking about revelation since Mansel's day, and then consider how, in consequence of this change, we have been forced to modify our way of understanding the significance of the person of Jesus Christ. For I think, with some measure of assurance, that in this place none of us is prepared to go the extreme lengths of the modern "followers" of Mansel; and hence, for good or for ill, we are bound to come down in one way or another on Maurice's side of the controversy of the 1850's. Somehow or other, revelation must be universal, in that something of God must be known to all men by the very fact of their being human and being possessed of the capacity to respond in an evaluating fashion to the world in which they live. Christianity, we believe, granted that it has its special assertions and its unique convictions, must yet be set in that context —otherwise, in the last resort, it will be found to be *absurd*, and absurd in a way very different from that intended by Tertullian in his celebrated adage or by Kierkegaard in his effort to confront men plainly with the mystery of "the Eternal coming into existence in time." But the Christian faith has never been understood as absurd in the pejorative sense; it may have been an offense to man's selfishness, pride, and sin; but it has never been considered a stark outrage to everything that his best and most chastened reason can discover or know. On the other hand, few of us would wish to say, with the older orthodoxy, that

Christianity rests essentially on biblical or ecclesiastical dogmatic propositions.

What do we mean by revelation?

It is here that William Temple made his most significant contribution to Anglican divinity. In his celebrated Gifford Lectures, *Nature, Man and God*, Temple defined revelation in what has become a famous phrase, "the coincidence of divinely guided event and divinely guided response." It is of course not to be thought that Temple was alone in moving the understanding of revelation from propositional statements to historical events as these have been apprehended by human agents. The movement of thought generally known as neo-orthodoxy, associated primarily with Karl Barth, had been traveling in the same direction, although here the reaction was not so much from propositional revelation, whether biblical or ecclesiastical, as from the rather vague liberal Protestant notion that revelation consisted essentially in the inspiration and illumination of man's inner life. But Temple's discussion in the Gifford Lectures and his further treatment of the theme in his beautifully compact essay in the symposium *Revelation* were the most notable Anglican, and indeed Anglo-Saxon (if I may so phrase it), contribution to the change in view. Furthermore, Temple's way of stating the position had the special merit of allowing a genuine place for the reality of human response, thus avoiding the apparent relegation by the neo-orthodox writers of the creature in the revelatory situation to the position of a mere "sounding board" for the voice of God speaking through events.

Revelation, then, is not centered in propositional statements, however true these may be. Neither is it given simply in the religious life of men who in some fashion are possessed of spiritual insight and understanding. Essentially, revelation is an action-reaction complex. Events which occur in the public domain are apprehended in their deepest meaning by those in whose presence they take place. The events are seen in a dimension deeper than that of surface happening; and the response which is made to the events is more than a mere acquiescence in their occurrence. For the events come to be understood in the light of what is already conceived to be a divine purpose working itself out in the historical realm, while the response is such that the beholder is caught up into, brought to participate in, or (to use the Tillichian phrase that has become popular in recent years) feels "grasped" by the events as they make their impact upon him. And the two—occurrence and response—are, as Temple said, coincident; the event and the apprehension are not to be separated, even though they must be distinguished one from the other.

The view of revelation which I have so briefly characterized is now accepted, with whatever qualifications, in almost all responsible theological circles, both in the Anglican Communion and in the English-speaking world in general. Perhaps it has been accepted almost too uncritically, for as it seems to me, there are certain very important modifications required in it if it is to be maintained as true. To those modifications—or, perhaps better, those further aspects of the revelational situation—I shall turn in a moment. But at present I should like to make it clear that the past 150 years have brought us to what is in fact a quite new position in respect to the basis of Christian faith in revelational event. In Mansel's day, and for a long time afterward, the important thing about the event of

Christ was not so much that he had lived among us, had undergone certain experiences, and had been obliged because of all this to think and act as a man in a given time and place and under particular circumstances, as it was that the fact of his having thus been with us was given a specific theological interpretation. In other words, what mattered most was not the fact of Christ, but the dogmatic description of that fact. The actual life of Jesus had given rise to the dogma of the Incarnation; the dogma was itself the revelation. The death of Christ, with its consequences for human experience, had occurred; but the central point was that this demanded, and had received, sufficient statement in the dogma of the Atonement. And so also with the other elements in the traditional Christian dogmatic scheme, whether this was interpreted by Catholic or Protestant, by Roman or Anglican, by Calvinist or Lutheran.

I am oversimplifying, of course, but yet it is the case that what is today called the thrust of the position common in 1817, and for a long time thereafter, was in *that* direction. Now it is very different. The event, the fact, the historical occurrence—these are given the priority, and whatever theological statements may be necessary to interpret their meaning will be secondary. Temple himself understood this very well, for he insisted that there are no "revealed truths"; rather, he said, there are "truths of revelation." By this he meant that there are inductions from those events and from the response made to them, such as will most adequately convey their meaning in the eyes of faith. But since the "truths of revelation" are thus secondary, they cannot claim the kind of fixity which in an earlier age was regularly affirmed in respect to dogmatic statements. They are subject to change; they may be developed, deepened, broadened, even critically evaluated, as succeeding generations wrestle with them and work through once again the process by which the dogmas came into existence in the first place.

When George Tyrrell, in a celebrated essay, distinguished between the revelation of God that is Jesus Christ, which he considered to be *semper eadem,* "always the same," unchanging because historically grounded, and the theology of the Church, which not only is open in principle to modification but also in fact has demonstrably undergone such modification, he was making much the same point as that which in another way Temple brought plainly before us. What, then, is the way to discover the truth in the Christian enterprise? Here we are brought to another area of thought in which there have been similarly vast changes in the past century and a half. The next lecture will concern itself with some aspects of that problem.

But I return to the qualifications—or, better phrased, to the further aspects of the meaning of revelation—to which Temple perhaps did not give sufficient attention. I shall mention three of these aspects. First, the absolute necessity for a prior view of nature and history that is essentially prophetic in quality. That is, we require an interpretation of the world which sees it as the sphere in which a divine purpose is being worked out; or, to put it another way, there must be an acceptance of the Old Testament perspective as a necessary precondition to any interpretation of the event of Christ as being in fact supremely revelatory of God. Second, a recognition of the patent fact that such a supreme event-response complex as is found by faith in Jesus Christ and the apprehension of his significance is, from one point of view, "dated." It took place at a particular time and place, and hence what is required, if the continuing Christian faith is to be made possible for succeeding generations, is some agency by virtue of which what occurred in the past can be seen as also a present reality. Third, as a consequence of this requirement, the necessity for a recognition of the Christian Church, of Christian worship (especially of eucharistic worship), along with the scriptural record, as the means by which the response once made in the past is communicated to the present while at the same time a "repetition" of that response, with all its particular and special qualities, is made possible for the modern Christian believer. About this last point, Temple himself was much concerned, for on more than one occasion he is said to have insisted that what our Lord "left behind him," after the days of his flesh, was a community of believers in whose continuing life he was himself present in the world.

Let us make some comments on each of these three matters.

I. First, it seems to me clear that whether or not any particular event or constellation of events will be interpreted as being in fact an activity of God in self-revelation will be determined by the particular preconceptions with which one approaches the event or events. If one has already accepted a view which is basically "naturalistic," in that it regards the world as nothing more than a purposeless confusion or at best a process of purely mechanical activity, it is apparent that one will hardly be able to speak of any specific occurrence in that sort of world as in any sense revelatory of God's activity. If one has adopted a world view which sees nothing but a continued repetition without any novelty, and hence without the possibility of points of particular importance, it is clear that no given instance can have revelatory significance, although one might speak of the total enterprise as being in the broadest fashion a disclosure of some rather impersonal divine reality behind or in it. In such a view, every instance would be *equally* important and, hence, for practical purposes, equally unimportant. Again, if the position adopted before considering any specific event were pantheistic, so that the term "God" meant nothing more or other than the total series, the specific event under consideration would indeed be *one* of the series, but could hardly be seen as focally significant. If one's preconception were that God is a remote or absentee ruler who retired from the creation once he brought it into being, the approach would be so deistic that the only way in which some particular occurrence could be interpreted as specially important would be by regarding it as unique in the most absolute sense. It would be without intimate relationship to the general run of events in the created order; hence, it would be a catastrophic intrusion into the world, and far from disclosing the basic meaning of that world, could only make nonsense of it.

On the other hand, if one accepts what I have called the prophetic world view, in which God is both the creator of the world and also the ever-present operative power working within it and through it—never exhausted by his activity in creation, always moving through it to accomplish the purposes he has in view, for the accomplishment of which the creation in fact exists—if one accepts such a view, then given events and given constellations of events can be seen as the occasions for greater or lesser, more complete or less complete, more adequate or less adequate disclosures of the undergirding purpose. Hence, they would be revelations of the nature of the divine Reality, who in this process is manifesting himself in a world which is not identical with him, yet is the sphere of his most intimate operation.

This correlation of an earlier and, so to say, wider view of the world with the specific claim made for a given particular event explains, I think, the insistence of early Christian theologians on the necessity of the Old Testament as integral to the Christian interpretation of the significance of Jesus. These theologians understood, although doubtless they would never have put it in just this way, that without the prophetic interpretation of the world which the Old Testament provides, the figure of Jesus would be at best an intrusion, essentially unrelated and meaningless, into the creation; it would not be a disclosure of the meaning of the whole creative enterprise. Tertullian's well-known attack on the position which was associated with the name of Marcion is indeed nothing less than a sustained argument for the basic unity of the Old Testament and the New Testament at precisely this point. To speak of some creator-god who is not also the God revealed in Jesus is to refuse to give Jesus a significance that will make him revelatory of the very heart of reality itself. But if one is to see him as thus revelatory of the central truth about things, one must of necessity see him against the background and in the context of an interpretation of the world apart from his appearance, an interpretation which makes sense of that appearance and which at the same time gives a basis for saying that there we know, with a new clarity and in a new focus, what God is *always* up to. The faithfulness of God is at stake here.

2.   But it requires more than the prophetic interpreta-

tion of the world and of history to make possible the evaluation of Jesus' appearance as the "divinely guided event" central to our understanding of the truth of things. It also requires that the event plainly take place in the realm of ordinary historical happening and, in that sense, be a public event, not some esoteric secret occurrence, "done in a corner," as St. Paul said. Further, the initial response to the event, in which it was seen as a specific disclosure of God's activity, must in some fashion be made available for succeeding generations, so that they too may enter into it, feel its proper impact, and by their being put in the place of the first witnesses, know it for what it is. That is to say, there must be a communication of the past event-response to make it come alive in the present. Otherwise it will remain perhaps an important, interesting fact in the distant past, about which we may have some information and concerning which we may make a second-hand judgment; but it will not become an "engaging" fact in our contemporary experience. When Prof. John Knox tells us that the Christian Church can be described as the community that "remembers Jesus," he is entirely correct; but it is to be noted that in order to account for all the facts, he is obliged to combine with that statement about the Church another statement which is equally true— namely, that the Spirit of Jesus or the Spirit released by Jesus' coming is the inspiring and sustaining Reality in the Christian community. The Jesus of history *is* none other than the Christ of the Church's continuing life, known through the spiritual insight which links the contemporary fellowship with its own past—the Spirit who in his profound impact on the company of believers is seen to be divine in his own right. "No man can call Jesus Lord but by the Holy Spirit," it is said; and in the specific connection that is our present concern, this means that without the continuing identification and the never-failing "coming-alive" in the present moment of the apostolic response to the initiating impact of the life of the historical person, Jesus would be known as a great prophet and a noble ethical teacher, but not as the living Lord in whom at a given time and place a revelation of God was made in a specific and adequate sense.

3. But what are the agencies by which this making present of the past event-response is accomplished? Here the Scriptures and the Eucharist have their unique place in the total Christian picture. By familiarity with the New Testament story of Jesus, by entering into the primitive response made to that story and to the person about whom that story is told—in other words, by meditation on the Gospels and the epistles and the other New Testament literature—and by seeing that story and its response in the context of the Jewish interpretation, both of history and of nature, as the sphere of the divine self-expressive action and, hence, of the divine self-disclosure, the succeeding ages of Christian believers are enabled to be participant in the story and its response. The familiar Negro spiritual asks, "Were you there when they crucified my Lord?" The answer is "Yes, I was there, when I read about it in the New Testament and saw the Crucifixion in the light of the Jewish hope for God's supreme self-revelatory act in reconciling his world to himself; I was there when I read the story with such opening of the self to its meaning, such meditative pondering of its import, that it spoke to me as more than a historical record, as so much more than merely such a record that it became a 'lamp to my feet' and the 'master light of all my seeing.' "

Yet the Scriptures, in isolation from the Eucharist, would always be in danger of lapsing back into *mere* history, in the sense of a chronicle of events in the past. Through the eucharistic action, in which the Christian community finds a genuine communion with the Jesus about whom the Gospels speak—and that a communion of very special and intimate quality—the response in self-commitment and obedient service is effectively made possible. Whatever may be our theoretical explanation of the meaning of the "presence" in the eucharistic action, with its "remembrance" of the events which gave rise to the Christian faith and made possible the Christian life in grace, the basic fact of it remains unquestioned. All Christians, save for the Society of Friends and the Salvation Army, have found that the Lord's Supper is the way in which Jesus is best known as with us in our present experience. In the lovely Lucan story of the post-Resurrection walk to Emmaus, we are told that Jesus expounded to his companions the things said about him and about his death "in the Scriptures"—which in that immediate situation meant, of course, the Old Testament, but which for our purpose must include the total biblical story. But we are also told that "he was known to them in the breaking of the bread." In the common meal, with Jesus present as their host, they came to know him for what he was, the One "who should have redeemed Israel," the One who in very truth *had* redeemed not only Israel but the whole family of men. We can say with assurance that it has been the wisdom of the Christian tradition to put together, with unfailing discernment, the two modes in which the historical event in the past, in which Jesus was known through the apostolic response to be the very action of God, is made a living and present fact in the life of Christians in the ages which followed that dated and located occurrence.

It is often said, although I think not accurately, that Anglican theology has concerned itself much more with the Incarnation than with the Atonement. Those who make this claim, or advance this criticism, are likely to go on to say that the reason for the supposed concentration of Anglican theology on the person rather than on the work of Christ is to be found in the inveterate Pelagianism of the English-speaking Anglican Christian, who cannot take with sufficient seriousness the appalling sinfulness of man. On the other hand, the Continental theologian, it is said, along with his disciples in other parts of the world, including English-speaking countries, is keenly and painfully aware of man's condition, and hence must concern himself with the way in which, through the work of Christ, God has provided a remedy for sin. As I have said, I do not think that Anglican theology can be charged with an exclusive emphasis on Incarnation, for I recall the enormous amount of writing on the Atonement in our theological history, from Reformation divines like Ridley, Latimer, and Cranmer, through the Carolines with their strong sense of man's willful rejection of God, to the Evangelical Movement and the almost morbid concentration on sin and the need for redemption in some of the early Tractarian leaders. What can be said, I think, is that in Anglican theology the Atonement has usually been seen *in the context* of God's presence in Jesus Christ—a point which in our own day a distinguished Presbyterian theologian (George S. Hendry, in his *Gospel of the Incarnation*) has said is essential if we are to avoid an inadequate and unbalanced understanding of the meaning of Christ. In this respect, Anglican theology resembles the strain in the patristic age, perhaps the strongest strain in that age, which with Athanasius in the *De incarnatione* quite simply refused to distinguish sharply between Atonement and Incarnation. It was the "Word by whom all things were made," said Athanasius, the Word whose *organon,* in his own phrase, was the whole created cosmos; who in Jesus Christ "became man," making a human life his *organon* in a special and focal sense. He alone could conquer death and corruption and restore man to his divinely intended nature, precisely because creation, incarnation, and redemption, as Athanasius saw, were all parts of a single process of divine action and of providential concern for the human race, all effected by that Logos, or Word.

However this may be, there can be no doubt that the christological question has been among the more important theological interests of Anglicanism during the past century and a half. Four books may be mentioned as indicating this strong concern. First there is H. P. Liddon's Bampton Lectures, *The Divinity of Christ,* delivered at Oxford University in 1866 and published the following year. Here we find a sustained, deeply Christian defense of what Liddon took to be the traditional Catholic teaching. The lectures are hardly very original in approach or presentation, but they are insistent on the necessity of the two nature-one person christology, and illustrate this doctrine with a wealth of patristic reference. As one reads them today, one is disturbed by the presence of a quasi-Apollinarian idea of the divine knowledge of the Incarnate Lord, an uncritical acceptance of the dominical miracles precisely as they are reported in the Gospels, and a rejection of all attempts to go behind or beyond the formal Chalcedonian statement.

But we ought not to be surprised at this. At that time, and given the kind of mind that Liddon possessed, we could hardly expect anything else.

In the second book to be mentioned, however, we find a great advance. This volume is Charles Gore's Bampton Lectures for 1891, *The Incarnation of the Son of God*—a discussion which four years later Gore supplemented by another work (*Dissertations,* 1895), in which further problems of a christological sort were honestly faced if not satisfactorily solved.

Charles Gore was in the Tractarian tradition, but he did not have the rigid sort of mentality which so markedly characterized the earlier leaders in that movement. He described himself, in his old age, as a "liberal Catholic" who valued the adjective as much as the noun in that description; and for him this meant acceptance of biblical criticism, openness to philosophical, scientific, and sociological influences, and a keen sense of the necessity for emphasizing the humanity of Jesus. We may feel that he accepted biblical criticism only up to a point, but we must admit that he, more than any other Anglican divine, made it possible for such criticism to be incorporated into the generally orthodox theological structure. Even if his development of a peculiarly English version of the Continental theory of a kenotic Christ does not appeal to us, nonetheless we must be grateful that he refused to minimize in any way the full reality of the humanity of the Lord. His kenotic theory is, indeed, marked by many serious difficulties—it seems to assume a strange mythological transaction in the heavenly places, by which the Word sloughed off his metaphysical attributes while retaining his moral ones; and we cannot avoid the question whether a deity so depotentiated can in fact still be called unqualifiedly divine. Even the later, and more carefully formulated, kenoticism of Oliver C. Quick in his christological chapter in *Doctrines of the Creed* (1938) may not be acceptable today. Yet we must recognize, and gladly affirm our thankfulness for, the effort which Gore and, later, Quick were making to secure that the Lord whom we worship is also seen as the Brother of men; and we must honor their sure conviction that, as R. C. Moberly said in his great work *Atonement and Personality* (1901), it is only when the Incarnation is seen as a presence and activity of God under genuine conditions of manhood—not other than man or apart from man, but in man and as man—that the Incarnation can really make any sense. They insisted on this truth, however much other theologians seemed unwilling to allow fullness of human nature in the Incarnate Lord, with all the limitations which such fullness may imply and yet with all the richness which it reveals as deeply intentional in the humanity God has created.

Liddon thought about the Incarnation in the familiar propositional terms of his time; Gore understood that the dogma of the Incarnation is a theological statement whose significance is found in its adequacy to describe the reality of the Incarnate Lord as a living, active, saving Person. Quick went beyond this, and he was able to do so because the recognition of revelation as divine activity rather than as information given in statement had at last been generally accepted in the theological world. That it was accepted among Anglicans was due, to a large degree, to two important books which are among the last I wish to mention: Lionel S. Thornton's *Incarnate Lord*, published in 1928, and William Temple's *Christus Veritas*, which had ap-

peared four years earlier. The almost simultaneous pub-
lication of these books is significant, for it means that in
the mid-twenties of our century, the influence not only of
the new view of revelation, which Temple was to work out
in detail a decade later, but also of evolutionary thinking,
was being felt strongly in Anglican theological circles. This
evolutionary understanding of the universe had for some
years been slowly permeating the thought of Christian
scholars, but Thornton and Temple were among the first
to use it boldly—although not *the* first, for, among others,
J. F. Bethune-Baker had been working along these lines
for at least ten years, and even earlier such theologians as
Henry Scott-Holland, J. R. Illingworth, and Aubrey Moore
had written their essays in *Lux Mundi,* which Charles Gore
edited in 1889. These four should be given due credit for
exploration of the relationship of evolutionary thinking to
Christian faith, and specifically to the doctrine of the Incarnation.

Thornton was philosophically a disciple of Alfred
North Whitehead, and his huge book is a sustained attempt to rework christological doctrine in Whiteheadian
terms. Temple was emancipating himself from Oxford
idealism when he wrote *Christus Veritas* and was under
the influence of the philosophy of "emergent evolution,"
as found in such philosophers as Alexander and Lloyd-
Morgan. I mentioned these and other evolutionary philosophers in the last lecture. Whatever we may think of
Temple's and Thornton's books, we can only be grateful
for their concern with evolution. Especially today, when we
observe a return on all sides to an evolutionary world view
(one thinks of course of Teilhard de Chardin, but some of
us would think, rather, of the remarkable revival of White-

headian "process thought"), Thornton's and Temple's efforts deserve our closest attention and study. Temple's book is the more satisfactory, largely because it does not fall victim to Thornton's strange insistence that at the central point of the Incarnation we must desert the categories of emergence and process, and find there an insertion of the totality of the Divine Activity or Word into the ongoing created order. Thornton calls for this in order to secure the uniqueness and finality of Jesus; yet uniqueness and finality could just as readily, although along very different lines, have been secured by the careful use of the very categories which Thornton deserted. The result, in Thornton's case, is that we are given a sort of quasi-Eutychian interpretation of Christ, whereas Temple was ready to make the perhaps startling affirmation that if *per impossibile* the Word, in his special presence and action in Jesus, were removed from that total personal life, we should still have a man, genuinely personal in quality. Temple desired above all else to maintain the full manhood of Jesus, and he did not conceive the Incarnation so much as an "intrusion" as the fullest and final instance of the Divine Activity which undergirds the whole cosmos and is operative in every man by virtue of his creation in the image of God.

These, then, are the four books; but I must now mention one other—a book that has been neglected in recent years but merits our consideration and study as the best, because it is the most consistent and coherent Anglican christological effort of the last thirty years. I refer to Charles E. Raven's unfortunately named work, *Jesus and the Gospel of Love* (1931). The first section of the book is an attempt to maintain the Johannine authorship of the Fourth Gospel, and we may find this unconvincing; but the remainder of the volume is a thorough, if brief, treatment of our Lord as the One in whom the Divine Word, God in his outgoing self-expression, is focally present and decisively at work, yet without contradiction of his pervasive and universal presence and work in the whole creation and in human history and experience. Revelation is seen as activity, requiring spiritual discernment if it is to be accepted; the evolutionary perspective is wholeheartedly accepted and interpreted as providing a setting for this specific act of incarnating Love; and the necessity for the Christian fellowship, with its Scriptures and its sacramental worship, is maintained with vigor, even though Raven is highly critical of the institutional Church's failure in discipleship and its frequent refusal to let the Spirit of Christ move freely through its forms and practices.

This lecture must not conclude without a brief word about the christological approach and the christological interpretation which seem to me to be in line with those basic to Thornton and Temple, in agreement with Raven, and consistent both with the New Testament and with Christian experience, and also with the insights of the general philosophy of process to which I am committed. I have already attempted such an exposition in *The Word Incarnate* (1959). It will suffice to say that the change in our understanding of the meaning of revelation from that common in the first third of the last century, coupled with the picture of the universe and of man which we owe to scientific investigation, demands of us a further continuation of the labors of Thornton, Temple, and Raven. The person and work of Jesus Christ are at the heart of Christian faith, and we cannot fail in our effort to come to an understanding of the significance of the Lord in whom we have found life. In our day, that significance must be stated in the context of the world seen as a dynamic processive movement. I believe "process philosophy" is here our best resource. Yet Jesus' uniqueness and his decisive position cannot be surrendered by believing Christians, although our way of stating them must be very different from those of our forebears. The work must be carried on, in the confidence that since he is the revelation of the truth, nothing that is true will diminish his importance and centrality. For we know him to be the central clue to the nature of things.

4

The Church and the Christian Tradition

In this place it would be a work of supererogation to spend much time in a discussion of the enormous change in thinking about the nature of the Christian Church which has taken place during the past 150 years. The General Seminary was founded at a time when Hobartian High Churchmanship, with its slogan "evangelical truth and apostolical order," was exerting its influence on Episcopalianism in this country. The spirit of the General Seminary during the early days of its history was largely the product of that influence, Bishop Hobart himself being one of its first professors and president of its faculty. This was before the Tractarians had inaugurated their publications at Oxford, but when the "Tracts for the Times" made their appearance, faculty and students at the Seminary were deeply interested and even found themselves involved in controversy because of that interest.

Since those early days, the Seminary has seen the

Anglican Communion—as it came to be called later in the century—growing more and more conscious of its Catholic heritage. It has also seen the renewal of liturgical worship, first expressed in a somewhat uncritical borrowing from other communions and more recently in an awakening to the real significance both of primitive practice and of its own liturgical traditions. This awakening is the result both of the labors of scholars in many lands, some of them Anglican, and of the concern of parish clergy for an adequately traditional kind of worship which will also be appropriate and significant in our own day.

Nor need we devote time to the change in attitude, not only of Anglicans but also of Christians of many other allegiances, toward the nature and meaning of the Church's ministry. We can observe a considerable development from the somewhat wooden conception of "apostolical order," which marked the period of the Seminary's founding and prevailed in the late nineteenth and early twentieth centuries, to a dynamic and vitalistic view which sees the Church's ministry as the functional representative of Christ in his mystical Body—a view which was first presented with particular vividness and remarkable insight by R. C. Moberly in his neglected classic, *Ministerial Priesthood*. This book was first published in 1897 and (granted the modifications made necessary by historical and biblical scholarship since that time) is still perhaps the best treatment of the subject. Because of the change on the part of "high" Anglicans from emphasis on tactual succession to insistence on the representative functioning of the ministry, coupled with a more Catholic view of ministry in other circles, the possibility of some understanding with non-Anglican communions has become brighter, the significance of the episcopate has been given another and more primitively Catholic slant, and the whole question of ministry is now being discussed in broader and, I venture to say, more Christian terms.

But there are two matters to which I do wish to give attention. One is the relation of the Church, once it is understood in biblical terms as the Body and Bride of Christ, to the concerns and problems of secular life and society. Here both the shift in emphasis and the quite remarkable change in approach are worthy of very close study. The second topic is the significance of the continuing Church tradition in relation to Christian faith and the criteria for affirming the truth which is embodied in that continuing tradition. I believe that this area of study is of great importance. I shall discuss these two matters in this lecture.

But before I begin, there are one or two preliminary considerations to which we should give attention. The first, which I only mention here, since the next lecture will deal with it in some detail, has to do with the wider problem of the relationship of the sacred and the secular. The question of the relationship of the Church and society is best seen as a concentration of the larger issue of the relationship of the sacred, by which I mean that which directly and specifically speaks of, and relates men to, the reality of God known, adored, and served in his self-disclosure; and the secular, by which I mean that whole area of human experience in which God is not directly and specifically seen and known. It seems to me quite wrong to consider the Church-society question in isolation from the sacred-secular issue; and I believe that one of the most gratifying developments in recent times has been the recognition of the close connection of the two.

The second preliminary consideration cannot be treated so briefly. We are all increasingly ready to "take time seriously," as Leonard Hodgson used to say many years ago, when he taught in the Seminary. Because of the new awareness of the social character of all human experience, which we owe to the work of psychologists, sociologists, philosophers, novelists, and many others, there is a much more general recognition that man's social past largely determines his actual present. No longer is it possible for anyone to think of himself as a kind of "window-less monad" or to talk about human individuality as if it meant that each man is a discrete, insulated, and isolated instance of humanity. We know that we all belong together; we are all bound up "in a bundle of life," as the Old Testament phrase has it; we are all inescapably what our past has made us—and this applies both to each and every man and to each and every society of men. Of course, this does not imply that we are helpless victims of our past; we are free agents and the societies to which we belong are capable of alteration, modification, and development. Yet it is widely understood these days, as it was not understood in most, if not all, circles a hundred years ago, that "history is the account of how we got this way." Frank Gavin frequently said that in his Church History lectures here in the thirties. Since this is true, our history *counts*, and it counts for us as social beings who live in and with our fellows, not only in the so-called secular world but also in our churchly association.

Let us acknowledge frankly, to begin with, that we do live in a secular society. We live in a society in which most of the physical and many of the cultural needs of men are provided for, not through ecclesiastical agencies or religious organizations, but by the State itself. Even in Britain, despite the establishment of the Church of England, and, in its measure, the Church of Scotland, society is ordered essentially on secular lines, not through churchly institutions, while in other countries—the United States, for one, not to mention the officially "secular" society of India and most other lands—there is no official recognition whatsoever of Christian faith. And we know that in some parts of the world—Soviet Russia and China, for example—there is a social structure which is definitely antagonistic to any religious faith. In most parts of the world, therefore, provision is made for meeting human need, government is exercised, and society is organized without specific and explicit religious sanctions—in fact, without the Christ whom we as Christians proclaim to be "the way, the truth, the life."

But is that really quite true? It will all depend on what we mean when we speak of Christ. If we have in mind the historical Jesus, the Man of Nazareth, the Incarnate Lord, it is true. But if we mean the Eternal Word, the creative outgoing activity of Deity, "by whom all things were made," by whom also all things are sustained, without whom nothing would exist and in whom all things hang together, then it is not true. And this (as we shall see in the next lecture) is part of the value of secularity. For it brings home to us most vividly and directly one aspect of the Christian faith which we so often forget: namely, that God works and moves, expresses and reveals himself, not only—and perhaps not chiefly—in strictly religious circles, in ecclesiastical institutions and practices, in theological concepts and liturgical exercises, but in the total creation —in all things that are made; and he does this through incognitos, under most various and often surprising names, and by most various and often surprising means. This rich background of the universal creativity and inescapable presence of God gives point and adds poignancy to what God does, as we believe, in the specific presence which he grants us in Jesus Christ as the incarnate Lord, the Man in whom God signally and focally acts for us men and for our wholeness, our salvation.

The point of the Christian Church, in this situation, is that it serves as the place and occasion where God in Jesus is known, worshiped, served, and obeyed. We call it Christ's "Body," by which we mean that in and through its continuing life the presence and power of Jesus, the Incarnate Lord, are made available to succeeding generations of men and women. But the Church is itself a strange paradox, for it is both the "sacred and wonderful mystery" in which Jesus unites us to himself and (as Dr. Tillich so rightly pointed out in the final volume of his *Systematic Theology*) also subject to the laws which govern all human groups. In other words, the institutional Church is both the Body of Christ and a society of men, with the limitations, defects, and liability to error and sin that mark any institution. So the Church is called, as William Temple used to say, to "become the Church"; the human institution is to become what it intentionally is: the place where God in Jesus is known and worshiped, served and obeyed. But this is not for its own sake, not that it may glory in itself, but that it may bring the secular world—the world in which God indeed works to accomplish his will of good, often through very secular agencies—to the conscious recognition, knowledge, and love of that very same God, brought near to us, made vividly real to us, in the Man Jesus.

I believe most of us today understand this, in a fashion different from that of our fathers in the faith. Further, we know that this task is still, even today, vitally important. Granted that God is at work in secular society wherever justice is sought and given, truth found, goodness achieved, love shared: granted all this, what we require because we are finite men and women is some focusing, some pointing of it, some decisive *there*, where we can be grasped and held by God in a manner which the secular ways of his working cannot and do not provide.

Once we have been grasped by the divine activity made real for us in Jesus, then we can see how relevant all this is to the affairs of men. The faith that in Jesus, God acts in love, is to be related to every corner of our human existence; we have been given a clue, a key, to the purpose of that human existence, and to the meaning of the natural world as well. To express this in worship by adoration and praise, and to express it in life by sharing in loving concern for our brethren: this is what Christians are here for. Thus the mission of the Church is simply to make Jesus available, so that the sheer goodness, the supreme excellence, he reveals may illuminate the secular society of our time as it has illuminated other societies at other times. Of course, the ways in which the Church must carry on this mission will not be the same today as they were fifty, a hundred, five hundred, a thousand years ago. One of the most pressing needs of our time is for hard thinking about the new ways in which that mission can be undertaken and the new ways of action in undertaking it. That is one of the things that most concern us today— and very rightly. But there are some other things that we can say at once.

First, it is becoming increasingly clear to us that we

cannot *use* Jesus, or the God he discloses, as a stopgap, as
if we possessed some device to excuse our human laziness
and ignorance, some way of evading hard thinking and
hard doing. God works in and through human agencies,
sometimes in spite of them; but he never works as a convenient substitute for them. And Jesus can never be "used"
as our excuse for not doing our plain duty of working at
the problems which face us: he helps us by giving us "a
master light for all our seeing," God as loving companion
and inspirer, and by strengthening our wills to carry on the
task when the going gets hard. We call that his "grace,"
by which we mean the enabling power which comes from
the dedication of ourselves to him as our Master, our Pattern, our Lord. Perhaps we should reread William Porcher
DuBose as he speaks of all this in his autobiography, *Turning Points of My Life.*

In the second place, we are able to see more clearly
what the gospel is all about. It is not an adornment to an
otherwise good and happy life, although it is vitally concerned that men shall have such; nor is it a political plat-
form, although it is vitally concerned with politics; nor is
it a substitute for welfare agencies, although it is vitally
concerned with man's welfare; nor is it a means of enter-
tainment, although it is vitally concerned with the joys of
life; nor is it an escape from sorrow, although it is vitally
concerned with sorrow; nor is it a way of evading death,
although it is vitally concerned with the fact that men die,
and dares to affirm that they will live again. The gospel is
the proclamation of the embodiment, the specific presence
in this world, of the reality of God. The Church speaks
of the ultimate concern which each and every man, each
and every society of men, in each and every time and place

in human history, must have with and for and in and toward that reality of God, who is the final environment, the inescapable given, the deepest structure, and the supreme activity. Failure to be related to *that*, in terms of the love shown in Jesus Christ, is man's basic disorder and maladjustment, the disease of man's soul, for which the medicine of the gospel is the remedy. Unless something makes this concern, this relationship, with the reality of God vividly present to men, human life becomes trivial, superficial, and ultimately meaningless and stupid. Our action is frustrated, and we become cynics, unless undergirding all we do and think and are is a relationship with that which is more than human, more than man and his ways. In the first flush of success in providing for the needs of men, this is not always seen. Yet in the long run, all such achievement becomes dead and senseless—which is why so many novelists and dramatists and poets today, lacking such concern, find human existence stupid and inane, "a tale told by an idiot, . . . signifying nothing." Man is made toward God; his ultimate subjective aim, as Professor Whitehead would say, is fulfillment in that which is more, grander, better than himself or any human achievement.

Third, we are increasingly aware, as our fathers often seem not to have been aware, of the danger of an idolatry of the Church. The Church's chief concern is the relating of all that men are and do to the great reality of God seen as love in Jesus. When it is interested in itself, suggesting that when the proper ecclesiastical motions are performed, it has done its job, resting in comfortable churchly ways and pleasant churchly thoughts, it becomes a horrible thing. We need to heed Frederick Denison Maurice's warning, given a hundred years ago, that the Church can "dose people with religion," in this sense, when what they cry out for is the living God, in relationship with whom they may know cosmic adjustment, cosmic healing, true order, and abiding dignity. It is the living God, known in Jesus, worshiped in faith, served with obedience in loving concern for our fellows, who can give final meaning and purpose to human life; and the Church exists to proclaim this, not to further its own institutional concerns.

Certainly it is true that in the devoted research of the scientist, the wonderful creativity of the artist, the dutiful labors of the wage earner and the homemaker, the joy of little children and the wisdom of old men, the brave acceptance of suffering, the faithful response of the dying, in all good things everywhere, in every spot where truth is revered or beauty enjoyed or goodness manifest, where justice is done, civil rights granted, men helped to live in peace and security—in all these, God is revealed. The Church is called to recognize this, to rejoice in this, to help men see and accept this. But beyond and above all this, undergirding it all, there is something more, something which secures men against despair, enables them to live with courage, and establishes them in deepest personal integrity. The Church's faith stands for and points to that something more: to God made present in the life of Jesus. It is the Church's supreme task in a secular society, where God is ever working incognito, to give that God a name; to declare in season and out of season that the Reality which men serve when they do justly and love mercy, seek truth and create beauty, is Love, the Love which was made flesh among us in the Man Jesus, the Love which by him conquers lovelessness and makes men whole. Having declared that, it is the Church's task to unite men with that

Jesus, through worship and life in obedience, so that they become in him what he himself ever is: man at one with God because God is at one with man, God living and working in man, so that man may live and work for the Love that is God.

We now turn our attention to the second topic, the continuing Christian tradition and the norms for establishing its truth.

On the face of it, tradition can mean either the act of handing over or handing down, *or* the "whatever it is" that is being or has been handed over or handed down. *Traditio,* as the act of handing over or down, is to be distinguished, therefore, from *traditum*, that which has thus been given to us. I rather suspect that a good deal of the disagreement about the meaning of the Christian ministry, for example, reflects some confusion of these two ideas; and it is certainly the case that the attack upon the whole concept of tradition, so evident in the days of liberalism, was at least in part a reflection of the same confusion.

But we still have the problem of understanding the nature of the *traditum*. Does it consist in a series of propositions, theological statements, defined liturgical practices, and the like? So it was understood by many divines in the last century. In that case, it was fairly obvious that the way in which such material comes to us would be seen as the logical development of certain ideas, the exact communication of formulas, the precise repetition of accepted ways of conducting Christian acts of worship. On the other hand, as is more frequently the case today, when the *traditum* is conceived of in a more vital fashion—as the spirit of the Christian past, say, which has been expressed in certain statements or practices but which is in itself a less readily defined reality—then it will follow that the manner in which it is thought to come to us will be more like the influence of a family's atmosphere or spirit. If we regard the Christian reality, in its wholeness, as a relationship with God known in Jesus Christ—that is, as a certain kind or quality of life—we shall have a feeling that the way in which this is communicated to us, and is made alive in each succeeding generation, is through participating in the communal experience and sharing sympathetically in its beliefs and practices, which is very different in feeling from the simple acceptance of particular formulations or the repetition of particular actions which have been customary in the ages that have gone before us.

I do not intend to enter upon any detailed discussion of these questions, although their statement is indicative of the changes in attitude during the past century. I shall give a definition of tradition, in both senses of the word, and then make some suggestions as to ways in which tradition so understood may be both tested and controlled. In doing this, I must of necessity assume that Christianity is an *identifiable* thing—in other words, that there are *some* assertions, *some* basic convictions, *some* attitudes, *some* modes of worship which (with whatever alterations or modifications may be found in phrasing or in expression or in implementation or in performance) are yet constant. I must assume that Christianity in the year 2000 will be recognizably the same thing, granted differences of a secondary sort, as Christianity today or in the first years of its appearance in the world.

By "tradition" I mean, first of all, the ongoing life of men and women, through succeeding ages, in a community or fellowship in which Jesus Christ is acknowledged as

Lord, in which he is understood as disclosing the inner nature of the divine Reality we call God, in which he is known to establish for erring and sinful men the authenticity and wholeness of life which they so badly need, in which those who share are knit together in genuine community, in which worship and prayer are directed to God through that same Christ who is still known as a living person with whom contact is possible, and in which through certain inherited communal actions (notably Baptism and the Lord's Supper) such a relationship is both initiated (in Baptism) and nourished and strengthened (in the Lord's Supper). That is to say, the meaning of tradition is basically the reality of a life in grace, which is also a life in relationship, a communal rather than an individualistic life. This life is communicated to succeeding generations by their being incorporated into the community which knows it and lives it. Furthermore, and as a consequence, the life is handed down and handed over by the participation of each new age, and of each new person in that age, in the communal life which is life in grace. Such communication is more biological and psychological—in fact, personal (which, I take it, means an open sharing, one with another, in social relationships)—than it is conceptual or logical. I do not wish to minimize the latter; I only wish to say that it seems to me that the heart of the ongoing Christian reality is handed on from age to age in a fashion more like that in which a family continues in self-identity than like that in which theoretical, speculative, or formally conceptual ideas are communicated.

Christianity is a historical religion in two senses. It is historical in that it is inescapably tied up with the events which as a matter of fact occurred in Palestine two thousand years ago and which are seen as a focusing of a whole series of happenings in which God was singularly at work to make it possible for Jesus to appear as what he was and to be apprehended for what he was. Christianity is also historical in that it is a positive faith which has its existence in a society which we have come to call the Church. Apart from that embodiment in a community, it is hard to see how it could have continued to exist as a live option for men down through the ages. Christianity is itself a *process*. In Whiteheadian terms, one might say that Christianity is a routing of a series of occasions, each joined to its past and each pressing on toward the future; it is constituted as an actual entity by reason of its memory of that past, its continual relationship to the world in which it is set, and its basic "subjective aim," which is the bringing of more and more persons, in more and more places, at more and more times, into a communally known, communally experienced, and communally shared life. In this way, to continue the Whiteheadian terminology, it is "important," in that it gives a clue to what has gone on in the world, enriches the present experience of men, and opens up for them newer and more expansive possibilities than otherwise would be available to them.

As a historical religion in the latter sense—that is, as a living community—Christianity depends upon the historical happenings from which it took its rise. That is part of the reason for the unique authority which in all Christian groups is given to the Scriptures. If you want to see what Christianity is like, in its essential quality, you must look to its formative years. These are reported to us in the New Testament, but that can be understood only when read in connection with the Old. What the Old Testament shows us to have happened prior to the appearance of Christ, within the nation and race in which he appeared, is significant because it made Christ, when he appeared, the kind of person he was; it is also significant because it was that long preparation which made it possible for those who companied with him and believed in him to apprehend him for what he was. The material in the New Testament, including Gospels and epistles and Revelation, enables us to see how in fact he was received, with the initial stages of that reception leading his disciples and their converts on to the apprehension of him as "the Word made flesh" in whom God was "reconciling the world unto himself." I suggest, therefore, that the first of the norms which must be employed for the "control" of the ongoing Christian life in grace, the *traditum* that has been "tradited," is the Holy Scriptures. Nothing may be required for acceptance as necessary to salvation, the various confessions of the sixteenth century tell us in their different ways, which cannot be "proved" by Holy Scripture. We must remember that "proved" is used here where we should use "tested." Hence, we may assert that basic to the Reformation witness, equally basic to the Eastern Orthodox witness, and now increasingly seen as basic to the Roman Catholic witness which today is undergoing its own reformation, is the recognition that apart from this scriptural test, there is grave danger of turning Christianity into an unhistorical mystery religion.

But we have yet to discuss the *way* in which the appeal to Scripture is to be made. Certainly it is not an appeal to the letter of the books; equally certainly, we cannot accept the notion that *only* what is explicit in Scripture can be believed or practiced by Christians. This kind of literalism would be the denial of the *vitality* which attaches to the tradition as life in grace. What seems our necessary procedure is very different from that literalism. We study the Scriptures in order to be grasped by the deep reality of God's action in his creation, to see this activity culminating in the action which is Jesus Christ, to catch the spirit which the primitive Christian community had known and which soon became for it *the* Spirit of enabling response indissolubly linked to the action of God himself. Thus we are enabled to understand the quality, the underlying reality, the essential nature, of all that Scripture has to give us—and everything is then to be tested by *that*. Here is no "fallacy of the perfect dictionary," religiously speaking; we are making an appeal to the formative period, the centrally "important" moment of the living tradition, in the conviction that in *that* period and *that* moment we can with certainty come to know what Christianity really is.

But the Scriptures are not isolated, either in actual fact or in the way in which they have been understood and used, from the community which treasures them as its most valued inheritance. On the one hand, unlike what was often taken as normative Protestantism, we cannot set Scripture over against the life in grace in all its richness, as if Scripture were some insulated volume without relationships and without consequences. On the other hand, we cannot separate Scripture and tradition, in the fashion of the older Roman Catholic theologians—and we may remark that the Council of Trent *sounded* as if it did this, no matter what recent Roman scholars may say about it. We cannot talk of Scripture *and* tradition, discovering in each equal authority in the life of the Christian fellowship and using one or the other as may seem desirable to us. The truth of the matter is that Scripture is itself a *part of tradition;* but it is, as I have said, to be taken as the normative, precisely because it is the formative, part. The extrascriptural part of tradition develops the implications of the normative, because formative, part. That is to say, it is the working out theologically and practically of what the scriptural witness tells us and establishes for us as essential to the Christian enterprise in its totality. This is how Scirpture was employed in the age of the Fathers. However we may differ in our technical use and terminology from that of Athanasius or Gregory of Nyssa or Augustine, to give but three examples, we can agree that they took the Bible precisely in this manner. And as John Knox has so eloquently argued in his *Early Church and Coming Great Church,* the first few ages of the history of the Church provide for us both a pattern for our own use of the biblical record and also a kind of indication, although not a final settlement, of *what it is all about.*

Since we belong to an ongoing process or a vital movement which is life in grace, in which our past is continually coming alive in the present and is projecting itself into the future, we do well to give our ancestors in the faith a vote in determining what Christian profession amounts to. The only way in which we can give them that vote is by listening to what they have to say; this we do by entering with deepest sympathy into their interpretations of the formative-normative Christian period. Perhaps this is why the Elizabethan canons set forth as standards for the doctrine and discipline of the Anglican Church both Holy Scripture *and* "ancient fathers and catholic doctors." Similarly, this may be why Calvin, for example, so regularly made an appeal to a whole series of patristic writers; and it may be why one of the remarkable accompaniments of the renewal of the Roman Catholic Church in our own day is a deepening awareness of and respect for the Fathers—not now interpreted in a wooden literalistic fashion but, rather, read in order to gain insight into their ways of apprehending and stating the central Christian assertions about God and Christ and Church and sacraments. Thus, I am suggesting that while the first, and in a special way decisive, norm is always the Holy Scriptures, a second and very important norm is the general tenor of patristic thought and practice; and, coupled with this appeal to the ancient Church, a respect for, combined with critical evaluation of, the whole historical development of the Church from its first days up to the present moment.

But to speak of the present moment brings us to a third significant point—and this has to do with our own contemporary experience of the relationship with God in Christ, of the life in grace which is in fact the meaning of Christianity. If the Christian reality were a philosophy, to be understood with the mind alone and accepted only for its logical validity, things might be different; but as a matter of history, Christianity is an ongoing life. Hence, we need always to see how some assertion which has been handed down to us, some practice which has been part of our heritage, is either confirmed or called in question by our contemporary spiritual experience.

I can best illustrate the point I am trying to make by taking one abiding Christian conviction and showing how it is "used," and thus tested and confirmed, today. The obvious example is the doctrine of the Incarnation, which formally states that Jesus Christ in the integrity of the total event which that name describes is both a man in the fullest sense of manhood and also the action of God in human life. He is both of these in complete personal unity, so that we have to do not with a schizophrenic, but with a truly integrated, personality. I am not concerned here with the minutiae of christological inquiry, for whose importance I should be prepared to argue; I am concerned only with the basic assertion about Jesus Christ which has been handed down from generation to generation of Christians, in the community of Christian fellowship, as one of the elements historically constitutive of the identity of the Christian reality itself. What do we do with, what do we do about, this assertion?

There are three things that we do. First, we accept the assertion because we know that it has been effective in ruling out ways of looking at, thinking about, and relating ourselves to Jesus Christ which would have the tendency drastically to alter some aspect of his continuing importance in Christian life. We see that to regard him as *only* a man, even if he were the best man who ever lived, would seriously damage the inescapable Christian assurance that in him and through him a kind of relationship with God has been established which is peculiar to the Christian life in grace. Again, we see that to *minimize or deny* his humanity and regard him as nothing other than divine act would make that action of God in and through him irrelevant to our human condition; he would be at best a strange visitor to our human condition, or he would resemble (as the Bishop of Woolwich has aptly put it) some human father who temporarily dresses up as Father Christmas but is not *really* what he appears for the moment to be. This would seriously damage the abiding Christian relationship with God established through and in one of our own kind. Finally, if we looked upon him as (so to say) a split personality, in whom now God and now man were seen as active in the world, we should be implying that the enduring reality, which we know in the ongoing life in grace, of union or communion with God in manhood through the person of Christ, was in fact only an illusion or at best a sporadic and indecisive affair. Whatever may be our formal christological statement, we can readily recognize that we need to accept the insight which the doctrine of the Incarnation provides, if we hope to continue in the tradition which historically has been known as Christian.

But second, this doctrine of the Incarnation has a certain regulative quality. By this I mean that it indicates to us that we are to take toward Jesus Christ the attitude which we should take to one who is truly man, in that Jesus is our Brother, while at the same time we take toward him the attitude appropriate to one whom we can adore, in that he is also our Lord. We do this by seeing in him, recognizing at work there, and opening ourselves to, the influence of the action of God which is prior to all human response. God comes first in him, as he always does everywhere; the response which Jesus as man made to God is the consequence of the divine action but, because it *is* response, is necessarily secondary to the action which evokes it. Hence, in the integrity and unity of the person whom we encounter in the New Testament, we find both the redemptive activity of God in man and the responding activity of man toward God; and this is seen in one person in whom divine action and human response are interpenetrative and intertwined. So we regard Jesus as that One in whom "God has visited and redeemed his people" but also as the fulfillment of manhood and the true pattern of human life. The life in grace is informed by and receives its color from this attitude.

Third, the doctrine of the Incarnation is, in an even deeper sense, indicative. It points beyond our attitude and our way of response to the reality which Jesus Christ actually is in himself as he has entered into the ongoing experience of men. His personal bringing into genuine unity of divine action and human response, in the integrity of one human life, is therefore not simply our "value judgment" about him, although of course it must begin there; after all, even to speak of the doctrine of the Incarnation is to say that we are making an evaluation of Jesus Christ in the light of all he was and is, all he did and does. But there is more . . . and that more should be described, I suppose, as ontological in quality. Whatever may be our metaphysic—and I submit that every Christian age necessarily employs one, even if it is not always conscious of the fact and even when it disavows all metaphysical concern—Jesus is understood, in our successive moments of "spiritual life," or relationship to God through him, to be genuinely and most truly *of* that supreme reality (however we describe it) which we mean by the term God, just as he is *of* our own reality as men. He is *of both of these* in the integrity and unity of his historically concrete person as the One who walked in Palestine, died on the Cross, and is known as alive again in the joy of his resurrection.

The negative, regulative, and indicative meanings of the doctrine of the Incarnation find their validation in the life of the contemporary Christian, built on the scriptural materials as primary witness and developed in the thought of the ancient Fathers and of succeeding Christian believers down through the centuries of the Christian community.

But there is still something more: the moral consequences of Christian belief and practice. Acceptance of the central affirmations of the Christian community, participation in its worship, and opening of the self to the inflowing of grace through God in Christ have had and must always have results in the behavior of those who profess to belong to that community. There is an abiding Christian "style" of life. It is difficult, if not impossible, to describe this with any great precision; the saints have been strangely different from each other, while at the same time there has been something about them all which marks them as being specifically "Christian." Yet certainly it is the case that were there not such moral consequences, such general patterns of behavior in all their variety, we should hardly be able to speak, as we regularly and naturally do, of the identity of Christian fellowship and its effectual implementation in the circumstances of life in each succeeding age. Any belief, however right or however venerated, or any kind of worship, however beautiful or attractive, which fails to contribute to that quality of life in Christ, with its moral consequences, in what St. Paul called the "fruit of the Spirit," must be regarded with considerable suspicion; and if it becomes clear that such a belief or such a practice conduces to some result *other* than the kind thus characterized, we can be sure that something is very seriously wrong with it.

Finally, among those norms which control tradition, we must not fail to stress what can perhaps best be described as the appeal to reasonableness. As I said in the first lecture, there are some quarters, in early days as well as in our own time, where it has been fashionable to regard this appeal as most unsuitable for the Christian theologian. But I doubt if it can be asserted, with any seriousness, that Christian faith and practice have really been understood and commended with much success when they have been called "absurd"—and I mean this (as I said earlier) not in the Kierkegaardian sense, which is something very different, but in the vulgar sense of being plainly irrational and even offensive to the best, and most honest, thinking men and women in any age.

How we are to make this appeal to reasonableness is a matter for discussion; but that we must make it, as one of our criteria although *never* as the only one of them, seems obvious. Of any belief or practice which has been handed down or handed over to us, we must inquire not only whether it is confirmed in the continuing experience of men in their relationship with God in Christ, not only whether it produces moral fruit so that it reproduces the abiding quality of Christian discipleship, but also whether *it makes sense*—and this means whether it fits into, even while it may also correct and amend, the sort of interpretation of experience which honest thought "secularly" understood is prepared to give.

Let me sum up what I have been arguing for in respect to the contemporary idea of Christian tradition. Tradition is the business of handing on to succeeding ages the ways of believing and acting which are consequent upon accepting the biblical witness to God in Christ as normative and decisive. Its validity and faithfulness can be tested first by its loyalty to the over-all scriptural record, then by the willingness to see how in the formative years of the community's history this witness was understood. But it is essential to discover how far such a tradition comes alive in, and gives the peculiarly Christian quality to, the ongoing life in relationship with God in Christ in our own day and among ourselves. Furthermore, it is necessary to consider how any given assertions or practices produce or fail to produce the quality of life which is specifically Christian. Finally, we can never fail to consider to what degree, and in what way, the things which the tradition has to tell us make sense of, and give sense to, the general experience of men as they honestly and humbly seek to come to terms with the truths which every human discipline honestly pursued may have brought to light about the world in which the tradition finds itself, with its particular affirmations and its specific practices. I believe this is where we stand today in our view of Christian tradition as basic to Christian faith.

5

The Sacred and the Secular

In the preceding chapter, I noted that the problem of the relationship of the Church to secular society so much discussed in our own day is a focusing of a more general issue—the relationship of the sacred, by which I mean the direct and conscious relation of men to God and the ways and means through which that given relation is established and sustained, and the world in its secularity, by which I mean the areas of our experience and the understanding of the world in which there is not that direct and conscious sense of God. There can be no doubt that the pursuit of the ordinary affairs of life and the major daily concerns of men in their thought and action are not in fact consciously directed to God.

In most of the period of 150 years which we are considering in these lectures, the problem of this relationship of sacred and secular has indeed been a real one, but the ways in which it was treated in the past are quite different from those prevalent among us today. Either an attempt was made to sacralize the secular, so that religious matters were regarded as the only really important concerns, or there was a secularization of the sacred, in which the religious dimension tended to be dismissed as purely fictional or at least relegated to a very unimportant place in a man's life. Of course, it was never possible to work out in practice the full implications of either of these two extreme positions; I am speaking here of *tendencies*. The former tendency is well illustrated in a strange fact upon which Baron von Hügel once commented: that Dr. Pusey never found himself able to develop any interest whatsoever in things which were not specifically and obviously "religious." Von Hügel said that this attitude filled him with horror—and rightly so, we should all agree. On the other hand, those who in the nineteenth century styled themselves "secularists" took a very dim view of the whole area of religious interest. If they did not dismiss it out of hand as mere wishful fantasy, they thought of it as important only for the few who wished either to escape from the hard realities of the world as it really was or to find some little area where they could obtain comfort and strength to enable them to face life in its stark reality.

We are now living in a period when secularity, in one form or another, is welcomed by the most vigorous Christian thinkers of our day, while many of our so-called "secularist" friends are showing a surprising willingness to listen to those who, while recognizing and insisting upon the reality of the "non-religious," can yet give to it a significance or a meaning that redeems it from triviality and gives some sense of purpose in ordinary commitments to the affairs of the world. This may not be specifically religious, in the conventional meaning of the word, but it has a quality which Paul Tillich has taught us to call "ultimate concern."

In this chapter I shall attempt to sketch the position which seems fairly widely accepted among thoughtful Christian people today and which has been expressed in Anglican circles (although with differing emphases) by such thinkers as William Temple in the first half of the century and by John Robinson in our own time. This line which I shall describe is worth our attention for other reasons than that it is widely accepted among thoughtful Anglican writers. It merits our consideration because of its honest facing of the perennial problem while at the same time providing guidelines for practical solutions of particular issues as they appear to the ordinary Christian man or woman today.

We may best approach our discussion by noting that within the past few years we have witnessed a great revival of interest in the doctrine of creation. In the earlier years of our period, even among churchmen who like the early Tractarians and their successors in the last quarter of the last century were insistent on the centrality of the Incarnation in Christian faith, the consciousness of sin and the need for redemption were so much at the heart of Christian thinking that very frequently not much attention was given to the basic doctrine of the relation between God and his created world. It may seem odd for an Anglican to criticize other Anglicans for giving undue emphasis to the doctrine of redemption, since we are constantly charged with being Pelagian both in our preaching and in our theological attitude. Nonetheless, I believe it to be true that in the nineteenth century, both the Evangelical

Movement and the Tractarian Movement were concerned mostly with the fact of sin and with the only possible escape from condemnation for sin by a just God—the escape found in the atoning work of Christ. I am not minimizing the horror of sin or the need for redemption when I say that today, while most of us would be ready to admit, and indeed to stress, the reality of man's defection from his divinely intended nature, it is precisely the fact of defection *from* a given intention which is being stressed. As Dean Fosbroke once said to me in this seminary, much theology of the past century has been "a theology of desperation," concerned with how we can be got out of the appalling mess in which we have put ourselves, while he himself felt that what we needed was to take the Old Testament teaching on creation so seriously that our theology would be—and here I quote his exact words— "a theology of restoration, in which redemption is seen as a new act of creation."

Basic to the modern approach, then, is the emphasis on creation; and it is interesting that even such a strong Lutheran as Bonhoeffer protested against what he decried as "religion" because he felt that "religion" as he knew it put such an emphasis on man's wickedness that the fact of the goodness of God's creation and its capacity to disclose the purpose of God had been forgotten. Anglican theologians, like William Temple in the last generation and almost every contemporary Anglican writer who is now publishing popular or technical works of theology, begin their study with a consideration of the doctrine of creation and *then* proceed to say whatever they have to say about evil and sin. This is much more like the *general* biblical witness (including even St. Paul, I venture to say) than was the older line of approach. Nonetheless, it has become the convention, in many clerical circles, to condemn secularism as the chief enemy of what is described as "the religious interpretation of life." It is the duty, we are told, of all religiously or spiritually minded persons to combat this secularism with all their force, lest it destroy religion and rule God out of the universe. Now I wish to combat this view, as do the writers I have mentioned. Those who think and speak in this fashion have an inadequate, not to say false, conception of God and a sadly deficient understanding of his ways of working in the world. In fact, among the most serious enemies of *true* religion may be counted this prevalent idea that secularism is to be attacked and, if possible, destroyed.

There is indeed a sense in which secularism is the great enemy not only of the religious interpretation of human existence but of man himself. *If* by secularism we mean a metaphysical position which denies that there is anything beyond the here and now, the present immediacies of human experience; *if* by secularism we mean a narrowing and limiting of reality to that which can be measured and weighed—then there can be no doubt that secularism is the enemy not only of religion but of humanity itself.

Yet it seems that by secularism many in clerical circles all too often mean not such a metaphysical view but, rather, the attempt to study and describe large areas of human experience, and great tracts of the world in which that experience occurs, without reference to specifically religious or spiritual principles. The thing that they are attacking is not some ultimate philosophical interpretation, but the legitimacy and value of a kind of inquiry which is not explicitly and avowedly spiritual or religious. They use the word "secularism," and they invoke the evil associations which have gathered round that term, as a whipping boy for all our ills and as a compensation for their own failure to come to terms with the facts about man and the universe which modern inquiry (scientific and other) presents to them. It is my contention that they are very wrong indeed. For religion, in the sense in which all too often they mean it, is nothing other than a *demon*— a partial truth pretending to be the whole; and the true and only God, who is the Reality undergirding and penetrating through the whole derived creation, is forgotten or implicitly denied by them, even if in word they confess him and wish to proclaim him.

The position which I am taking, in opposition to all this, would claim that the so-called secular studies in which, for example, most persons in institutions of higher learning are engaged are not only legitimate studies in themselves, but also are concerned with areas of human inquiry which *ought* to be secularly understood and in which it is not only improper, but even blasphemous, to introduce specifically religious categories. It is integral to the Christian faith, historically understood, to insist that God is not only the Lord of the sanctuary; he is the creator, or, as we might say, the ultimate ground of all existence and the explanation of that existence in its every aspect. Whatever he may be called, he is the abiding Reality upon whom all that is not-God depends. He brought it into being, he sustains it in being, and he is actively at work in it. All too frequently, alas, religiously minded people have thought that God is "interested" only in churchly matters or in that which is specifically and narrowly "religious." But, as William

Temple once said, the probability is that God is interested in religion hardly at all, in this narrower sense, or at least interested in it only because religion (which is man's consciously directed attention to the divine Reality and his willed relationship with that Reality) is necessary to human life if it is to be full and whole, authentic and real.

Furthermore, it is integral to the Christian faith, historically understood, that as the creator and sustainer of the whole order of derived existence, God is concerned not merely with the salvation of men, with their relationship to him and their redemption from false self-centeredness, but is concerned above all with the expression of himself, his Self-Expression, if you will, in the world which he has made, is making, and will continue to make until his final purposes are accomplished. So much has this been part of central Christian thought that God's Self-Expression has been seen as a reality "consubstantial" with himself, as his outgoing movement not only in the created order of existence but also in the mystery of the divine life itself. The chief statements of that conviction, in the New Testament, may be found in the Epistle to the Colossians and in the first few verses of the Fourth Gospel. The Word, of which those verses speak and of which St. Paul also speaks in his own idiom in Colossians, is the Reality who is "in the beginning with God," "through whom the worlds were made," who is "the light that lighteth every man," who (in a fine phrase from St. Irenaeus) is "the measure of the unmeasured Godhead." That is to say, Self-Expression is so much part of the divine nature that it is in truth nothing other than God himself in his outward-going creative power. It is in this context that both the Fourth Evangelist and St. Paul—and with them the theology stemming from Nicea—see Jesus Christ; he is that point and place, that human life, in which this Word, this abiding Self-Expression integral to God himself, is most plainly and evidently seen, known, and at work, so far as manhood and human history are concerned. In him, as nowhere else among men, "the Word is made flesh" or "en-manned."

The point of this theological excursus is that there is no area, no place, no time from which, in Christian belief, the eternal Word of God—God in his outward-moving Self-Expression—is absent; hence, there is no area, no place, no time in which the reality of God is not operative and knowable. This is the theological basis for the Christian claim that the God with whom men have to do when they meet Jesus Christ (in whom God is declared to be manifest in human life, with singular clarity and fullness) is precisely the same God—for there is but one God—who is to be met in every range of human experience and in every field of human inquiry. This is the cosmic sweep of Christian faith; this is the disclosure of the meaning which is hidden, yet revealed, in the mystery of the creation. But—and this is a very important "but" —God is knowable in many areas, places, and times, through what I think we may properly call incognitos. He is indeed present and knowable everywhere; but he is not thus present and knowable in a fashion which would make it possible for us to recognize him at once under his proper name of Personal Love. This we are enabled to do when he is met in the specifically religious experience, and above all in the fellowship of Jesus Christ.

I can illustrate what I mean by recounting a personal experience. Some years ago I was present at a concert in

Carnegie Hall, New York, at which the famous Boston Symphony Orchestra, under the direction of the late Serge Koussevitsky, played Brahms's Fourth Symphony. During the *passacaglia* in the fourth movement, I found myself strangely moved—lifted out of myself, so filled with the glory of Brahms and the splendor of Dr. Koussevitsky's conducting that I knew what T. S. Eliot has described as "music heard so deeply, that it is not heard at all,/but you are the music, while the music lasts."

Something of the same sort of experience is known to all who love music greatly rendered; for me it was one of the high moments of my life. The next morning it suddenly occurred to me that this had been almost exactly what the mystics describe as a profound "religious experience." And I asked myself, "Why, then, did I not at once recognize that here I was truly in communion with God in all his beauty?" But a moment's reflection assured me that it was much better that *at the time of the experience*, I was right in *not* thinking in these terms at all. "For the fact was," I said to myself, "that God was revealing himself to me in his great incognito of Beauty; I knew him *sub specie pulchritudinis*—and it would have been wrong, it would have been blasphemous, to tear away the veil of that incognito." But then I went on to think that the fact that as a Christian I could say that it was in truth *God* who was in and behind all this, not only enriched the experience itself but also enriched my understanding of the glory, mystery, and wonder of the divine Reality.

We might, then, put it in this way: God chooses and uses secular incognitos. He is not only Personal Love, although that is his very heart; he is also Order, Truth, Beauty, Goodness, Courage, Integrity. He is the ground and final explanation of all things; but he accommodates his self-disclosure to the particular concerns and interests with which men seek truth, create and enjoy beauty, foster goodness, manifest courage, show integrity. He accommodates himself, too, to the particular ways in which, in given circumstances and under given conditions, he can best accomplish his abiding purpose of self-expression. He is known always *ad modum recipientis,* in St. Thomas Aquinas' great phrase; he reveals himself in terms of, and according to, the capacity of those to whom he would make himself known—and he does this in accordance with his own ends and his everlasting purpose of good in the world which is his creation. It is simply wrong, it is even blasphemous, for us to seek to break down, or break through, the incognitos which God thus assumes. It is precisely in and under those incognitos, in their very secularity, that at that time and in that given area of human activity God is to be adored.

There is the famous story of the astronomer LaPlace, asked by Napoleon if he had found God as he swept the heavens with his telescope. His answer, the story goes, was, "Sire, I have no need of that hypothesis." He was entirely correct in speaking in this fashion; for in his study of the heavens and his reporting of that study in his *Mécanique célestiel,* he was not concerned with, nor had he need of, God in the strictly religious sense—which was the sense intended by the Emperor in his question. As an astronomer LaPlace was concerned with the order of the heavenly bodies, their stately procession across the skies, the pattern and plan by which this could be described. Here was a divine incognito—God was revealing himself to LaPlace, as he does to any and every scientist, in terms of his immanent operation, the creative process and its description. God is not to be found at the other end of a telescope —nor is he to be found at the other end of a microscope. Baron von Hügel once said that the trouble with Sir Oliver Lodge was that he always seemed to expect to find God in his laboratory; *that* was not the place, the Baron noted, where God in the religious sense is to be found. On the other hand, as a man, not as an astronomer, LaPlace did have need of God, as did Sir Oliver Lodge. After he had done his proper scientific work, it would have been quite proper for him to appropriate the words of another astronomer, Kepler, and say, "I am thinking God's thoughts after him." It would have been entirely right for him to say, after the fact, that it was really the divine self-expression which he had been tracing. But *after the fact*—for otherwise, he would have muddled the categories, and the muddling of categories makes all into confusion.

Furthermore, LaPlace and every other man engaged in secular work needs God in still a deeper sense. He needs a relationship with God which is personal and immediate, religious in the narrower sense, for without that relationship he is in terrible danger of lapsing into a sophisticated animal who is very clever but very devilish, twisting and turning the power his knowledge gives him into exploitation for his own perverted ends. It is an abiding relationship with God, personal and immediate, which keeps man human—and also keeps him sane, lest he develop pretensions, megalomania, and come to regard himself as the center of all things, the hub round which the whole creation revolves, and so become demonic, hateful, frightfully dangerous to his fellows.

Those who are engaged in secular work are right in

doing so. It is proper for men to study chemistry and physics, mathematics, history, psychology, sociology, and the rest; to engage in art and literature and music—and to do all this without constantly attempting to drag in artificially introduced religious conceptions. And the more one is convinced of the reality of God and of a right religious relationship with him, so much the more one must guard carefully the autonomy which belongs, in its place and time, to the secular incognito which the divine Reality has here assumed. When a Christian who happened also to be a teacher of biology in a secondary school asked me how he could best bring God into his work, I replied, "By teaching biology honestly, not by dragging religious categories into your class sessions or into your laboratory demonstrations." For the incognito which God takes in such classrooms and such laboratories is exactly in the teacher's scientific integrity, refusal to "fudge" results, utter honesty; and in the subject matter under study, the glory and wonder of organic life as it can be studied and known under those given conditions. But there is yet more to say.

The person who is thus rightly engaged in secular activity is also a human being, and he needs the personal and immediate relationship with God which religious faith makes possible. He needs this, not in order to modify or change the procedures properly employed in his particular secular discipline, but in order that he himself may find full, wholesome, abundant life, delivered from narrowing of interests and released for authentic existence in a world which God made; he needs this also so that *after the fact,* when his secular work is completed, he may see more richly and understand more fully the many-sided wonder of the world which God made and informs and in which, through secular channels of self-expression as well as through specifically religious means like prayer and grace and sacraments, God is ever manifesting himself and working toward the accomplishment of his eternal purpose.

When Socrates at the end of Plato's *Phaedo* makes his lovely prayer to "Pan and all other gods who dwell in this place," he asks that he may be made *kalagathos*—all-harmonious within, as I should translate it. Socrates here came very near to the vision that the Christian should possess. God's many-colored wisdom, as St. Paul puts it, is so rich and wonderful that it requires a harmonious life to apprehend it in its splendor. It requires both the secular and the sacred. And the secular order, in Paul Tillich's word, is ultimately *theonomous*; it points to, bears its witness of, manifests the divine reality, just as really, under its incognitos, although not so fully—just as truly, but not with such intensity and immediacy—as the specifically religious. In other words, secular study and inquiry have a certain proper autonomy which we dare not deny or violate; yet that very autonomy is an incognito for God who in other ways, known through faith, manifests himself to men personally and more immediately.

Let me give another illustration of the sort of approach I am expounding. The historical study of the Gospels which tell us about the life of Jesus of Nazareth is a very difficult matter. To the historian, as historian, the question always comes: What does this study disclose? If he is also a Christian, there is a constant danger (and in much contemporary study of the New Testament, experts have fallen headlong into this pit) of thinking that the divine Reality in and through the man Jesus is plainly manifest. Certainly it is in such terms that the Gospels as they stand tell us about Jesus, through messianic and even divine categories. Yet the historian, as historian, must penetrate these interpretative categories and try to see what is behind them, if he can manage this difficult task. When he uses ordinary historical methodology and the usual historical categories (and if he does not, he is not a proper historian at all, but fraudulently or unconsciously smuggling in his own conclusions or those of the religious body of which he is a member), he will find sufficient data to speak of a Jesus who is indeed the greatest of men, certainly a notable prophet and teacher, and surely One who drew from men an extraordinary and overwhelming response. But he will find *a man*.

It is when the historical inquiry has been carried through with utter integrity, when the data have been sifted and their probability assessed, that the question will arise—and will not be denied—"Who is this man?" Then there is room, and ample room, for faith; then there is place, and ample place, for making one's own the proclamation of the Christian ages. Then there is the opportunity for entering into a willed relationship with this Man, for following "in the blessed steps of his most holy life," for finding in him that One who can redeem us from meanness, arrogance, pride, and every evil way, and for knowing him as the Lord in whom God is present and through whom God works, as nowhere else, for men. It is through commitment in utter trust and loyalty to this historical figure that modern man can come to recapitulate the experience of the first disciples; by associating with him as man, he can come to know him as the Man who is focus and center of the God-manward movement, as "God in man made manifest." Then he can be caught up into his life and made one with him, to his great good and to Christ's great glory.

Our Lord's coming to us was in the context of a world of secular interests and concerns, a world in which he lived to the very limit of his manhood. It was in that world and in terms of ordinary human experience, shot through with moments of divine illumination, that he revealed, to the eye of faith, the illimitable yet personal reality of the God who always and everywhere works among us, with us, and in us, even when (in our entirely proper scientific, historical, literary, aesthetic, and ordinary day-by-day labors) we do not see him face to face.

Such, it seems to me, is the way in which we should look at the relationship of the sacred and the secular, if indeed these old terms are to be retained and used at all in our time. In putting it in this way, it is something of a comfort for an Anglican to know that contemporary Anglican writers of such different outlooks as E. L. Mascall and John Robinson would agree in general with what I have been saying. All of us these days realize that this is *God's* world, if we believe in God at all; and none of us is prepared to take such a narrow view as that so often, even if not always, taken by our fathers, who far too frequently seemed to think that Christianity was more a matter of extrication of man from this sinful world than an instrument for recognizing God wherever he may be found present and at work in it, and hence an invitation to adore him in his rich and varied self-expression. But lest I do an injustice, let me close by repeating the famous story told of Father Dolling, the great London slum priest of the late nineteenth century. Whatever may be one's feeling about the main theological thrust or the liturgical practices of the successors of the Tractarians, it was they who went into the slums of great cities and served Christ in the persons of his humble, underprivileged, and needy human brethren. Dolling was much concerned with problems of sanitation—in the English idiom, with "drains." Asked why a priest of the Church should have this concern, he is said to have answered, "Because I believe in the Incarnation." How right he was! But he might have prefaced his reference to the Incarnation by some mention of the creation—so that his answer would have been, "Because I believe *both* in the creation of the world by God *and* in the Incarnation."

For one cannot really believe in the reality of the incarnating action of God in Christ unless he believes also, as Athanasius so rightly insisted in the *De incarnatione*, that God could indeed "come into the world" in Jesus precisely because he is *already* in the world in his creative and self-expressive activity. In the terms of classical theology, it is the same Word of God by whom all things are made who is incarnate among us in the Man Jesus. Christianity really knows *no* distinction, ultimately, between the sacred and the secular. It is *all* God's world, even in its evil and sin; God loves the whole world, the *cosmos*, as the Fourth Evangelist and the writer of I John put it. With this faith we can share the wonderful confidence expressed by Mother Julian of Norwich, when she tried to find an answer to the question of the meaning of the whole creation. She heard, in her "shewing," she tells us, God's own reply: that the world is what it is and as it is "because God made it, because God loves it, and because God keeps it."

6

The Anglican Tradition in Our Day

Much that has been said in these chapters about Anglican theology might have been said of many other groups of Christians who in the present divided state of Christendom make up the "Holy Catholic Church throughout the world." Yet I believe that it remains true that Anglicanism manifests a quality, a genius, which is distinctly its own. It has been placed by history in a position from which it sees the Christian faith and life in a special way. I say this, not simply because I happen myself to be an Anglican, but because I am convinced that anyone looking at our communion can see this peculiar quality of its faith, worship, and life.

The fact is that the Anglican Communion, in all of its branches throughout the world, is a synthesis—which, precisely because it is a synthesis, is *not* an amalgam—of diverse elements which in separated form are found elsewhere in Christendom. This is of course one reason for the strategic position which Anglicanism has occupied until

quite recent years in the movement toward Christian re-
union. It is also—and this is our interest in this last lecture
—the reason why the enterprise of theological reconstruc-
tion seems to have been a continuing part of its tradition.
For Anglicanism's deep sense of history, of institution, and
of sacrament has removed a fear of losing moorings when
it seeks to restate the faith, while its essentially liberal
spirit, which I believe is derived from the long history of
English religious humanism, has delivered it from simple
acquiescence in tradition for tradition's sake. Above all, its
firm allegiance to the primitive Church Fathers and its
recognition of the differences among them has made it
possible for a distinction to be accepted between what the
King's Book of 1536 called "things necessary and things
indifferent"—a principle which in Anglican theology has
been carried much further than the King's Book intended.
It is appropriate, therefore, to close with a consideration of
the "spirit" of Anglicanism.

The really distinctive thing about Anglicanism is not
to be found in any particular set of beliefs or way of
worship, but in the fashion in which Anglicans live, believe,
and worship as members of the Universal Church. The
Anglican Communion is neither one among several varieties of Catholicism, nor one among several varieties of
Protestantism, but a particular way of being a Christian
which is in principle inclusive both of Catholicism and of
Protestantism, but inclusive also of much else—and notably
of the liberal spirit in thought, the humanistic spirit in
practice, the capacity to discriminate between essential
and unessential matters, which in fact marked the great
Fathers of the Anglican Church in the sixteenth and
seventeenth centuries.

Doubtless we Anglicans are irritating to many of our

fellow Christians, by reason of what they think to be the internal contradictions in our *ethos*. But that shows only that these critics have not been able to understand the spirit which animates us. Doubtless we are the despair of some who would have us come down flatly on one side or the other in many of the divisions which run through Christendom today. But this shows that our critics do not see that there is something about that Anglican spirit which makes such an apparently simple step an utter impossibility for us. Indeed, the only way to understand what Anglicanism *is*, is to understand, in words of Dr. Frank Gavin that I quoted earlier, *how we got this way*. There is no Christian communion which depends so much upon its historical development as an explanation of what it is in its essential nature.

It is in this connection that the link with England becomes most clear. Today, as things stand, that link is of very slight importance; but historically, the spirit of the English people and their peculiar way of entering upon a reformation in Christianity is the key to the understanding of what Anglicanism has come to be. Let us look first at the simple facts.

Despite the erroneous statement made in so many school textbooks, we all know that the Church of England was not "founded" by Henry VIII. That rather extraordinary Tudor monarch played his part in the series of events which separated the Church of England from Continental Catholicism and which began the process of development from which the Anglican variety of Christianity took shape. But for years before Henry had his quarrel with the Pope about matrimonial affairs, England had been uneasy in its relationships with Continental Catholi-

cism and, above all, with the Bishop of Rome. In a sense
this may be said to go back even to the relation of the
ancient British Church, presumably founded very early in
our era, to the mission sent in the sixth century from Rome
by Gregory the Great. To any who are informed on the
history of Britain, the simple mention of the long controversy over the payment of *annates* and the authority of the
Church in relation to the authority of the State, the enact-
ment of the Statute of Provisors and Statute of *Praemunire*,
and like facts, should make plain the strange combination
of religious and political disagreement between Englishmen and their Continental fellow Christians, and more
especially between England and the Bishop of Rome over
what were felt to be usurpations of power by the latter.

Henry's matrimonial adventures provided the occasion, but they did not furnish the cause, of the rupture
which occurred in his reign between the Pope and the
English Church. And when the break did finally take place,
it met with general approval from the people of England;
otherwise, even with Tudor despotism behind it, it could
never have been carried through and maintained. The
English reformers left no doubt that they did not intend
to depart in any essential matter from the historic Christian and Catholic Church. The ancient creeds, the ancient
sacraments, and the ancient ministry were all carefully
preserved; the structures of historical Christianity, if I
may so describe them, remained as they had been. And in
later years, when attacks upon these were made by other,
dissatisfied Englishmen, the great body of the nation explicitly repudiated any action which would destroy the
structures or imperil the continuity which they secured.

It is quite wrong to suppose that the English Reformation was accomplished in a matter of days or even of a few decades. As my former colleague, Prof. Powel M. Dawley, has pointed out,* the Reformation in England took from the 1530's to the 1660's—rather more than a hundred years. There were certain notable incidents in this process—such as the declaration of independence from Rome, in Henry's time; the refusal to submit once again to Roman power, with the resulting excommunication of Queen and realm, under Elizabeth I; the slow consolidation of the Anglican Church during the days of the Stuarts; the "times of trouble" in the Commonwealth period; and the restoration of the Church at the return of Charles II to England. But throughout this period, the historic faith was preached and believed, the apostolic sacraments faithfully administered, the ministry by episcopal ordination continued; and, as recent studies in English parochial history being carried on in Cambridge have demonstrated, the ordinary life of the ordinary Englishman in the ordinary parish—and very often also the incumbency of the local parish priest—went on without too much disturbance —through one change after another, yet with no loss of the sense of belonging to the Catholic Church.

But of course something had happened with the Reformation in England. It was not merely that the claims of the Pope, conceived to be historically false and theologically impossible, were denied. More important, the specific insights of the Continental reformers were incorporated into the ancient Catholic structure. Roughly, these insights were three. First, there was the appeal to Holy Scripture as the "proving ground" for all doctrine;

---

* *Chapters in Church History* (New York: The Seabury Press, 1950), pp. 171–73.

hence the phrase in the Articles of Religion, to which I referred in an earlier lecture, that the affirmations of the creeds are to be accepted because they can be "proved" or "tested" by "most certain warrant of Holy Scripture." The Anglican way of being a Christian came, thus, to include a particular and strong emphasis upon Scripture, its theological value, its importance for study, and the need for patterning the Christian life upon a scriptural view of the true end of man. Second, there was the insistence that "justification"—which is to say, our being accepted by God in Christ—is through God's gracious action, received by his children in humble self-commitment or faith. This put an end to the whole machinery by which it was formerly thought that man could in some sense "earn" his place with God through religious works, however these might be conceived. And third, the English Church took to itself the Reformation emphasis on personal moral responsibility before God and the right of the individual to appropriate for himself, rather than through some agency acting for him, the religious truths which are the heritage of the Christian Church. This carried with it the corollary that no external authority could supplant the personal response of the believer, however valuable and essential such authority might be in a more restricted and edificatory sense.

But most important of all was the development of a liberal or humanistic attitude toward matters of Christian faith and life. This is a change which cannot be attributed to influence from the Continental Reformation divines; rather, it was the result of the religious humanism which had flourished in England during the late fifteenth and early sixteenth centuries. The names of men like John Colet, Dean of St. Paul's; John Fisher, Bishop of Rochester;

Sir Thomas More, Lord Chancellor of the realm; and Erasmus, the Dutch humanist who spent much time in Britain, will indicate the nature of this humanism. The change which its continuing impact on English religious life and thought brought about was in the direction of a certain liberalism, in the right sense of that much abused word. It meant a concern for humane studies, for a spirit of honest and open inquiry, for a trust (not naïve and uncritical, but chastened and devout) in the capacity of human reason to know something of the truth and to love and serve it, for a moral life which (in the phrase of the Book of Common Prayer) would be "sober, righteous, and godly," but yet not narrow and rigorist.

We can see all these things—the ancient structure of historical Christianity, the Reformation insights, and the liberal spirit—in many of the divines whom we call the Carolines; but their attitude has its roots far back of the seventeenth century in which they lived; it was seen in the earliest days of Anglicanism after its break with the Roman See.

As we have seen, when the English Church in the sixteenth century broke its bond with Continental Catholicism, it did not intend to destroy the continuity of tradition with the ancient Catholic Church. And again, when friendship was established with Continental reformers and their churches, the divines of the English Church did not intend to indicate by this friendship that they accepted all that they held and taught. If any proof of this statement were needed, a reading of Richard Hooker's *Ecclesiastical Polity*—certainly the classical statement of the *ethos* of the Anglican Church in terms of post-Reformation thought—would settle the question. Anglicanism is in fact *sui generis,* and there is no reason why Anglicans should be ashamed of the fact.

Professor Bethune-Baker wrote these words in 1927:

The Anglican Communion was refashioned by the march of events and the peculiar genius of the English people, in such strange wise as to preserve its continuity, and retain all the characteristic features of historical Christianity, while adapting in various ways its constitution and teaching to the new conditions and ideas of the time. So it found itself established in the unique position in Christendom that it has occupied since, and occupies today: Catholic and Protestant; primitive, medieval, and reformed; respecting antiquity and all that we call "tradition", but not inaccessible to fresh knowledge and new movements; tenacious of "the faith once delivered to the saints" but claiming no infallibility for the interpretations even of the most august assemblies of the faithful in the past. . . . By its history, by the very personality and character its special experiences have developed in it, it seems to be marked out as the destined representative of an organic Christianity continuously developing and shaping itself anew to meet the constantly changing conditions of knowledge and thought and life that determine for men the real world, generation after generation, that confronts them.*

We Anglicans, then, have no reason to be ashamed of our peculiar kind of approach to Christianity. It is not the only way in which a man can be a Christian; but those of us who have sought to understand and appreciate its special quality are glad to confess that for us, at least, it is the best way. We cannot judge for others; for ourselves, there is an almost intangible appeal about this kind of Christianity with which we are well content. And we have a suspicion that its particular *ethos* is not only valuable

---

* *The Way of Modernism* (Cambridge University Press, 1927), pp. 140–141.

and important for us, but is indeed indispensable in any rounded and balanced view of the Christian religion.

Many of our contemporaries are repelled by what seems to them the irrelevance of most of the older orthodoxies, including the Anglican ones. They dislike what they call its religious fascism; they are appalled by its refusal to come to terms with truth which is unquestioned in such fields as biblical criticism and modern science. But even in the period since this seminary was founded, Anglicanism has been changing; and an older kind of orthodoxy, which served well enough in its day, is no longer imposed upon us. On the other hand, many of our contemporaries have little sympathy with the moralism, emotionalism, and rationalism which they feel to be characteristic of much nonorthodox Christianity today. But Anglicanism has never been that sort of tradition. Many feel that they cannot enter with any enthusiasm into the dialectics of the recent "neo-orthodoxy" prevalent on the Continent, for it seems to them to be much more a paradoxically irrational exercise of the intellect than a working faith for busy men. But Anglicanism has not succumbed to this kind of theology. It is perhaps to such contemporaries that Anglicanism makes or can make its greatest appeal. It has substance, but is not stolid; it is conservative, but not reactionary; it is liberal, but not inclined to relativism. But it is not only to intellectuals that Anglicanism can speak. It can speak also to the simple man who asks for a faith which will clothe itself reverently in symbol, yet not confuse the symbol with the thing symbolized; who asks for a religious discipline that makes demands on his life, but does not outrage his sense of proportion. The Anglican Communion, by reason of its historical genius, can present the

Christian faith and life in understandable language and with the possibility of full participation in its worship.

I know full well that all this may seem very egocentric —as if we were proudly boasting of ourselves and condemning others. But the point is that Anglicanism is not our own invention; and therefore we cannot and do not boast of it as if it were. It is precisely the historical development of the Anglican Communion which gives it whatever claims it may be able to make; contemporary adherents of the Anglican way teach and practice a faith which is not theirs alone, but which comes to them through a long history into which they have been allowed to enter.

Anglicanism has often been described as the *via media*, the middle way between Catholicism and Protestantism. This idea was popular during much of our century and a half. But as it was commonly stated, it would appear to be simply false. Anglicanism is not a *via media* in the sense that it seeks a middle road between other versions of Christianity. It seeks to be an *inclusive* way, in which the significant emphases of Catholicism and the significant emphases of Protestantism are held in unity along with the significant emphases in the humanist tradition. This is unity in tension, for there are many stresses and strains within the Anglican Communion, not least among Anglican theologians. There are those who are inclined to give particular weight to the Catholic element or to the evangelical note; there are those who are strongly insistent on the religious humanism which has ever been found among us; there are those with a particular concern for personal religion and those whose main interest is in the social implications of Christianity; there are mystics and sacramentalists, intellectuals and activists. Indeed, one can never know just what variety or combination of interests one will find in any individual Anglican or, indeed, at any one moment in the life of a given branch of the communion.

But underneath them all, holding them in unity, is the combination of sound conservatism and sane liberalism. If Anglicanism is Catholic, it is Catholic with a difference; if it is evangelical, it is evangelical with a difference; if it is liberal, it is liberal with a difference. That difference is explained by the simple fact that into Anglican history there have entered so many strains that what emerges is something which is a unique expression of Christianity.

Historically this was indeed the result. The severance from Roman obedience was brought about not only by political considerations; it did not arise simply from resentment at what were felt to be the pretentious claims of the Roman See; nor was it just another reflection of the pervasive spirit of the Reformation. It was all these, but it was more. It was the result of Christian humanism in the fifteenth and sixteenth centuries just as much as it was a protest against the "enormities" of the Bishop of Rome and a reassertion of the Gospel message. The Anglican Reformation was not accomplished in a day, a week, a year, or a decade. It went on, as we have seen, from the first half of the sixteenth century to the second half of the seventeenth century. Into that whole stream of development, with its high points in the dissolution of the link with Rome and in the restoration of the Church under Charles II, there entered further intellectual, moral, and practical emphases which finally created the Anglican *ethos*.

It is for this reason that Anglicans have an imperative duty to be themselves. They must learn, in this ecumenical age, from other types of Christianity. To learn in this way has been one of the peculiar qualities of Anglican history. But Anglicans dare not be mastered by any given theology or practice from which they have learned and which they may rightly value. It is as much un-Anglican to make Karl Barth a theological lord as it is to make one of St. Thomas Aquinas. It is as much contrary to Anglican spirit to ape the fashions of Roman Catholicism as it is to copy the newest ideas of European Protestant thought. Anglicans have their own tradition; and they will never accomplish the task which has been given them if they barter away that heritage.

This lecture has had for its main purpose the insistence on the peculiar quality of Anglican Christianity. By this I have meant neither a self-satisfied neglect of what others are saying or doing, nor a proud insistence on our own special righteousness. Nor have I meant the teaching of this or that Anglican divine, whether in the sixteenth or seventeenth century, the 150 years we have been considering, or in the most recent suggestions concerning theological restatement. Rather, I have meant a willing adherence to the Anglican spirit, in which conservatism and liberalism are held in balance by the constant appeal to Scripture, history, reason, moral consequences, and religious experience. The main line can readily be traced, not least in the years since 1817, when this seminary was established. It might be summarized in this fashion. Anglican theology holds firmly to the essential faith of the Church, but recognizes that the faith must be reconsidered and restated from time to time, as occasion demands and need arises. The final court of appeal for this theology is Scripture interpreted by tradition and tested by its reasonableness, its moral results, and its spiritual fruitfulness.

But our newer understanding of the Bible has made imperative a change both in our manner of using it and in our grasp of what is central in it. Anglicanism during the past century and a half has been learning this. It has learned how to study the given tradition; with all humility, to employ our human reason to understand and to state it; it has also learned that it has the right and duty to take part in the developing of tradition, provided it does not negate or minimize the gospel that God in Christ was reconciling the world unto himself. It has come increasingly to understand that all knowledge, from whatever field it may come, is man's to use, for all knowledge (once it is tested and found worthy) is the gift of God and will illuminate the faith by which the Church lives. It has come to see that something like this is what we mean when we say that Anglicanism is a unique, because it is an inclusive, variety of Christianity. But lest we seem too theological, let us remember that all this has for its purpose the fulfilling of the Church's mission, which is to relate men, including modern men, to God in Christ. So I shall conclude with some words once spoken by Canon R. D. Richardson, who thus describes the Church:

The existence and the inspiration of the Church lies in [the] one vocation of Christ's disciples to show him forth and to work out the implications of his way of life, to be steadfast in its hold on the Reality whose nature he disclosed and on the sacraments which link earth to heaven. Real Christianity, because it is the religion of both Incarnation and Redemption, hallows all our life and makes it dedicate to God; it blesses our family ties, and strengthens our souls at their departing; above all, it constantly renews and transforms our every action; and it is centered in memories of a historical Person, in memories of his sufferings and triumph. And all this it is the function of the Church to set forth and to mark with its ministry, so as to teach it and make it available for every man, woman and child who comes within its system. Its creeds are intended as signposts to the nature of Reality. Its worship is practised with techniques whereby souls are released from the constraints of effort and of solitude and plunged into the rich life-currents of a great tradition. In the performance of the symbolic acts of baptism, confirmation, marriage, prayer and Eucharist— which are not only symbols but effectual, grace-evoking sacraments —it is the Church's task to nurture souls and educate the moral and intellectual powers. In private and in public life the Church [leads] men unerringly to God.